I was a student at Hope College from 1995 to 1999, so this memoir is, among other things, the story of my college experience. I had a front row seat—sometimes literally, sitting in the front pew at Dimnent Memorial Chapel—for many of the events (good, bad, and ugly) described in these pages. Ben Patterson was a formative influence in my Christian walk and ministry.

Some of my favorite memories in life are of listening to Ben preach the gospel so powerfully as Hope's chaplain. Ben is a man of deep prayerfulness, biblical courage, good humor, and energetic pugnacity. All of these traits come out in Ben's retelling of his controversial, painful, extraordinary, and fruitful years at Hope College. I'm grateful for Ben and for this book.

Kevin DeYoung, Senior Pastor,
Christ Covenant Church in Matthews, North Carolina

The account of God-moved revival you are about to read is true to the core. It really happened. God knows that the joy and pain recorded in this memoir stand as a testament to how the Almighty One moves through generations of faith-filled prayer and the hearts of people who are willing to follow God no matter what the cost. It also testifies to the power of God being unleashed even when there is skepticism, fear, and calculated resistance.

I bear witness as one who had the honor of preaching a number of times on the campus of Hope College during this season of revival and prayerfully supporting the Chapel Team as they navigated this holy work of God's sovereign hand and the complex repercussions that erupted because of it. Through it all, Jesus revealed Himself as Lord and ruler of all, to this very day, and forevermore, Amen!

Rev. Dr. Kevin G. Harney, Lead Pastor,
Shoreline Church, Monterey, California, and president of
Organic Outreach International

My lifetime study of spiritual awakenings and their extraordinary positive impact on the church and culture has conditioned me to, in fairness, also look for negative aspects that inevitably occur when these special happenings take place. The truth be told, through the centuries religious revivals have tended to be somewhat volatile and messy events involving strong, opposing personalities with deeply held opinions or convictions. Specific illustrations can be pointed out in the book of Acts in Scripture, during the Protestant Reformation, and also in the two Great Awakenings in our early American history.

Ben Patterson's riveting account of what took place on the campus of Hope College in Holland, Michigan, in the last decade of the twentieth century is a classic, recent example of such polarization. This illustration also is easier to get your mind around because of its more limited scope.

What could have been a "puff piece"—telling only the positive things that happened—is instead a truly helpful example of what life might be like if God answers the current prayers of his people for another "heaven-sent" revival. What's the old saying? "Be careful what you ask for!" Amid the overwhelming good, there is all too often a powerful negative reaction that also occurs.

I read Ben's manuscript the day I received it. The next day, I read it through again. Would you believe I laughed out loud this second time around at his humor, even though I knew what was coming. I also confess that I teared up over Ben's candor, humility, authenticity, and wisdom . . . and I prayed that God would use this honest book in our current times in a way far and beyond anyone's imagining.

Dr. David R. Mains, retired broadcaster, author, and minister

To Evan!

WHEN GOD SHOWED UP

Ben Patterson

Also by Ben Patterson

The Grand Essentials

Waiting

Serving God

Deepening Your Conversation with God

Prayer Devotional Bible

He Has Made Me Glad

God's Prayer Book

Muscular Faith

Praying the Psalms

Praying the Psalms Devotional

WHEN GOD SHOWED UP

A Memoir of the Surprising Work of the Holy Spirit at Hope College 1994–2000

Ben Patterson

credo
house publishers

Published in the United States of America by Credo House Publishers,
a division of Credo Communications LLC, Grand Rapids, Michigan
credohousepublishers.com

ISBN: 978-1-62586-269-3

Cover and interior design by Believe Book Design
Editing by Elizabeth Banks
Cover painting by Joel Schoon-Tanis

Printed in the United States of America
First Edition

To all who will come after us at Hope College—
that they may know that the Lord is God.

Posterity will serve him; future generations will be told
about the Lord. They will proclaim his righteousness to a people yet
unborn—for he has done it.

Psalm 22:30–31

The LORD has established his throne in heaven and his kingdom rules over all. Praise the LORD, you his angels, you mighty ones who do his bidding, who obey his word. Praise the Lord all his heavenly hosts, you his servants who do his will. Praise the Lord, all his works everywhere in his dominion. Praise the LORD, O my soul.

Psalm 103:19–22

Among the stone and colored glass
the Word was lifted up.
Vaulted Grace
descended to heal
by His wounds—blood and might.
Our eyes downcast still said Yes.

In! came the Presence and His glory burned,
Healing solidified to calling—
It is for you to cry
Worthy!
We closed our eyes to the brightness
But our bones were strengthened.

And the angels waited, just inside the stone.
To see the highway of prayer
Being built
from Heart to hearts darkened,
But we started to see—
For thin is the veil
and bright His love.

Meg (Gustafson) Gregor '99

Contents

Foreword

Ben Patterson changed my life. I'm sure Ben himself would be the first to dispute that statement, or at least the phrasing. He would rightly point out that he wasn't the one who changed me—God did. And, of course, that's true. God is always the source of any real change. But what is equally true is that God rarely works alone. Most of the time, he doesn't act unless he can find a partner. He won't work until he can find an instrument to use. And at Hope College in the 1990s, that instrument was Ben.

Oftentimes, the role of this instrument is simply to "prepare a way for the Lord." That's what Ben did at Hope. He flattened some hills, filled in some valleys, and cleared a path. And then, something remarkable happened: God looked at that path that Ben had cleared, and he walked right down the middle of it.

I was there when it happened. And it split my life into before and after. Having grown up in a devoutly Christian home, I had known about God my whole life. Ben introduced me to a deeply personal God. It was during the events detailed in these pages that God became a someone, not a something for me.

During those years, I realized how much God cared for me and that he'd do anything for me. I also heard him asking if I was willing to do anything for him. And what I said to him was, "Yes. Wherever you want to take me, I'm in."

My experience was not unique. There were hundreds of others like me—people who, despite years of attending church, encountered God's presence for the first time sitting in Dimnent Memorial Chapel. It made us hungry for more. Having tasted and seen, we embarked upon a life of pursuing God's presence.

My hope is that the same thing happens to you as you read this book—that maybe, just by reading about what happened, you might experience God's presence in the same way that those of us living through it did. I believe it's possible. But for it to happen, there's one thing you must do: you must refuse to be offended.

Some people who lived through these events missed out on the blessing because they couldn't get past some stumbling block of one sort or another. Those same obstacles remain today. As you read, you may find yourself disagreeing with some of Ben's views. That's okay. You don't have to agree with him on everything to hear God speaking through him. Society today loves to disregard someone as soon as disagreement surfaces. But God does things differently. He often intentionally chooses a messenger who is offensive to us in some way just to test us—just to make sure we fall in love with the gift itself, and not the packaging.

The way Paul put it is, "We have this treasure in jars of clay." That's what Paul was, and that's what Ben is too—just a jar of clay. So don't get distracted by the jar. Don't waste time analyzing it, deciding whether or not you like it. The jar is not the point. It's what's inside that matters. And what's inside is the sort of treasure that, once you find it, you'll want to sell everything you have to buy.

That's my prayer for you. May you find the treasure hidden in these pages, and may you give up everything to make that treasure your own.

Matt Scogin,
President, Hope College

Preface
(Lost in the Archives)

Since my youth, O God, you have taught me, and to this day I declare your marvelous deeds. Even when I am old and gray, do not forsake me, O God, till I declare your power to the next generation, your might to all who are to come.

—Psalm 71:17–18

In the juvescence[1] of the year
Came Christ the tiger.

—"Gerontion," T. S. Eliot

T his hasn't happened to me very often.

Usually my sense of God's call comes very gradually over time, after a lot of ponderings and conversations, and then at some point in time crystalizes into a clear, "This is what I want you to do." It usually feels like slowly waking up.

But I can give you dates on this call, even specific times, and definite names and places.

Tuesday, August 20, 2019, at 7:45 p.m., EST—Part one of the call came in the form of an email sent from a person I'd never heard of, a Hope College student named Reed Hanson.

> Hello Ben Patterson! I am Reed Hanson, the Hope student from Austin, Texas who researched on the faith of Hope College this summer! I was so blown away by what you were able to do and accomplish in the 1990s when I read about them in the campus ministries boxes at the Joint Archives! Thank you for all of that. It was delightful and wonderful to hear about what the Holy Spirit did through you and your staff those days! Praise the Lord!
>
> Anyway, I heard that you're preaching at the Gathering this Sunday night, and I cannot wait to hear you speak! I would love to meet with you for coffee and hear more about the revival that happened

under your tenure; do you have a date in mind that works?

Let me know what works for you, and let's sit down together!

I don't remember answering that email. I soon forgot about it, and the name of the student who sent it.

Forgive me, Reed.

Thursday, August 29, 2019, at 5:00 p.m., EST—Part two of the call came nine days later. My wife, Lauretta, and I were at Hope College to attend the dedication of the new Campus Ministries house, the monumental van Andel Huys der Hope, grandly planted in the middle of the campus. An upstairs room was named after us: the Ben and Lauretta Patterson Prayer Room. Sweet.

There was an abundance of earnest thanks and praise to God for the people who had made this event and structure possible. All the expressions of appreciation were absolutely and utterly deserved, especially the van Andel family and the Boersmas. Twenty six years before, Max and Connie Boersma had donated the money to endow the chair of the Hinga-Boersma Dean of the Chapel. I was the first Hinga-Boersma Dean of the Chapel. What joy. What a privilege.

Ah, Max and Connie Boersma! Two more delightful and humble servants of God you'll never meet. Max was gentle and wise, common sense incarnate. You just felt more sane when Max was around. He and some Hope faculty met with me weekly for seven years to pray for the chapel ministry. Over donuts, of course. Connie made you dance inside when she was around. She sparkled and laughed and made bold declarations. Her favorite was, "I'm still fightin' the devil!" Love oozed out of her. Max and Connie were a perfectly matched pair. Their family a testimony of God's goodness.

But as I sat in the dedication audience and listened to the speakers and the prayers, I was struck more by what wasn't said than by what was said.

What was said was that something good happened, beginning in 1994. Generous giving. Good staff. Creative programming. Charismatic leadership. It could be charted on a graph: in 1994 chapel attendance spiked to overflowing, and has ever since. Thanks be to God. What God was thanked for in the dedication made perfect sense: put love, magnanimity, intelligence, and creativity together and you get a vibrant program. No mystery here, it's logical.

What wasn't said was the part the Holy Spirit played. Or any reference to revival. Or spiritual awakening. Or the supernatural. Or what Charles Spurgeon called "holy disorder"—the messiness of the old order being replaced by the new order, God's kingdom come. What God wasn't thanked for was the fact that what we witnessed and experienced in the '90s was far more than the sum of its parts. As students then liked to say, when "God showed up." My staff and I would sometimes be lauded for the explosive numerical growth and energy of what was happening. And I would say, "Don't congratulate me. I'm not a humble man, but I'm just not that good. Only the Holy Spirit can do this." C. S. Lewis and Charles Williams compared Christ to a lion. G. K. Chesterton and Thomas Howard compared him to a tiger. Whatever the beast, they are all unmanageable. Aslan is not a tame lion.

After the dedication service, my friend Trygve Johnson told me there was a student who wanted to meet me. Would I have time? The student's name was Reed Hanson.

Over the next few days Lauretta and I spent several hours with Reed, as he told us what I hadn't paid attention to in his original email. We've had many conversations since. But on that day, within a few hours, the two signs came together—what he had discovered in the college archives about the '90s, and my disquiet over what wasn't mentioned in the dedication.

I thought, the story of how "God showed up" in the '90s will stay lost and forgotten in the college archives unless someone tells the story. It seemed obvious that the Spirit was telling me I was the only one who could tell the story.

But what kind of storyteller? I'm not a historian, trained in the discipline of sifting and organizing the facts of events from all angles. I am merely a witness. I can only testify to what I saw and heard and did during those remarkable days. I take heart at being a mere witness, since Jesus always stands behind his witnesses. He will establish it if what I said was true. And he will wipe away what was false.

My approach will be mainly anecdotal. I will tell a story, recall a vignette that embodies other stories and issues during the revival, and expand on them. I will merely show and tell.

1

An Exclamation Point

(Or why I wrote this memoir)

When the LORD restored the fortunes of Zion, we were like those who dreamed. Our mouths were filled with laughter, our tongues with songs of joy.

—Psalm 126:1–2

There are moments in life when you're just glad you were there. You didn't need to play a role or pull a lever or push events. You felt blessed just to be there, watching it happen. For me, the events that unfolded when I was at Hope College were like that. An incredible revival. A season of renewal, a call to move out in mission. I think I could run through every finger and toe, just rattling off names of people who went into significant, full-time ministry as a result of what happened in those days.

—**Adam Barr,** Hope College student in the 1990s, on the occasion of the twentieth anniversary of The Gathering (2014)

Why did I write this memoir? And why should you be interested in it? There are three reasons.

The first reason is the fun part, so I'll start with it. I wrote it for joy. As the saying goes, a picture is worth a thousand words. So look at the painting that hangs on the wall of my study at home, and which you can see on the cover of this book.

The artist, Joel Schoon-Tanis, painted it from a snapshot of the crowd packed into Hope College's Dimnent Memorial Chapel at the Sunday evening worship service we called The Gathering, December of 2000. How many students were there exactly? We never kept attendance, but a ballpark estimate would be around 1,400, give or take a few hundred. Since 1994, this scene has been commonplace: standing room only in an unrequired chapel, four times a week, for twenty-five years, right up to the writing of this memoir in 2023. Previously, attendance hovered around thirty or forty out of a student body of 2,700. And that was on a good day. But since that time, something sacred and rather stunning has been happening in the souls of thousands of Hope College students and in the self-understanding of the institution itself.

You Wait and Wait and Wait

Even though I had heard about things like this happening in American history, and had prayed to see it personally someday, I was surprised when I did see it—on this scale, and so quickly and dramatically. When I arrived at Hope in 1993, I had been a pastor for more than twenty years, and my experience of ministry was mostly like farming: you plant, you water, you fertilize, and you wait for growth. And you wait, and wait, and wait. Sometimes there are bumper harvests, extraordinarily large results, but not usually. This was very frustrating for me in my early years of ministry. I identified with a pastor who wrote somewhere, "Wherever the apostle Paul went, there were riots. Wherever I go they serve tea."

The painting depicts one of the last chapels I preached in, just before leaving Hope College in December 2000. The painter, Joel Schoon-Tanis, includes something the photograph doesn't. With his usual vivid whimsy, Joel put angels in the rafters—messengers of God's holy presence, hovering over the service, unseen but felt. Many who attended those services would say that what we couldn't see was the truest thing about those services. To say that heaven came down in those gatherings would be almost right, but not quite. The truer thing was that we were raised up, joining a larger worship service in heaven.

There is something else about the painting that may not seem obvious. Just as significant as the angels and the presence we couldn't see is what the students are doing. I am standing behind the pulpit holding my Bible above my head. Hundreds of students in the sanctuary are also standing holding their Bibles above their heads, shouting declarations.

There's a story here. In September of 2000, my last semester at Hope, I spoke at a Presbyterian pastors' conference in South Carolina. The other speaker was a black pastor from Virginia, whose last name I sadly cannot remember. His first name was James, and he was a fiery delight. Before he preached to us he had us all stand and enact a litany his congregation recited every Sunday before he preached to them. He asked us to hold our Bibles over our heads and repeat after him—

James: "This is my Bible." *Us: "This is my Bible."*
James: "It is the Word of God." *Us: "It is the Word of God.*
James: "It is the sword of the Spirit. *Us: "It is the sword of t*
James: "I am what it says I am." *Us: "I am what it says I am."*
James: "I have what it says I have." *Us: "I have what it says I have."*

By now, we were laughing, a little self-consciously, because we were Presbyterians, after all. Some people were known to chide us as "God's Frozen Chosen" for our tendency toward excessive sobriety in worship. We would sometimes chide ourselves. But there we were, our Bibles held high, thawing with each declaration.

Then he paused, and exhorted us— "The next thing you say, you need to say with an attitude. A Holy Ghost attitude." We braced ourselves as he modeled the attitude.

Loudly and defiantly, he said, "Devil . . ." *We echoed, "Devil . . ."*
James: ". . . I am armed." *Us: ". . . I am armed."*
James: ". . . and you should consider me dangerous!"

You Should Consider Them Dangerous

As we repeated that last phrase, we applauded the Holy Ghost thunderously. And ourselves too, a little, for saying it. The Word of God is the sword of the Spirit.

When I got back to Hope to preach at The Gathering, I thought I'd try it with the students. Before I preached I told them the story of what the pastors did. Then I invited the students to do it too, just for fun, which they did, even more exuberantly and thunderously than the pastors.

I thought the litany that evening was the end of what I assumed was an amusing novelty. But the next Sunday, when I started to read the Scripture for my sermon, I was immediately interrupted by shouts from the congregation. They were holding their Bibles in the air and imploring me to do the litany again.

So that's what we did every Sunday evening for the rest of my last semester as dean of the chapel at Hope College. My time at Hope College couldn't have had a happier ending. A generation was learning to love the gospel and the Word of God.

So I say to the enemy of our souls—Devil! . . . They are armed, . . . and you should consider them dangerous!

Whenever I look at the Schoon-Tanis painting, I remember that in that earnest and merry crowd of young people, with Bibles held high over their heads was a junior student I didn't even know at the time—Matt Scogin. Matt is now the fourteenth president of Hope College, inaugurated on September 13, 2019.

What happened in the 1990s at Hope, and is still happening, is nothing short of remarkable and spectacular—a dramatic and massive work of the Holy Spirit producing conversions and spiritual renewal and a call to missions and Christian ministry on a grand scale. I call it a "revival," not only because the word is accurate, but also because it has been the common term used throughout American history for this kind of event. A "revival" at Hope was for years what many had prayed for. That's the proper noun I started to use as the title of this book, "A Memoir of the Hope Revival."

Dolores Sheveland, one of the great people I worked with during those revival years, thought that title was weak. She exclaimed, "You're not writing a memoir, you're writing an exclamation point!"

Point well taken. The story of the Hope College revival is a great story. I only hope I can do it justice.

A Bellwether

A second reason why you should read this book is that what happens in the academy is a bellwether—an indicator of what is to come in society. This makes the academy a significant, if not the dominant institution in the formation of a culture. Dr. Charles Malik wrote in *A Christian Critique of the University*:[2]

> "The universities . . . directly and indirectly, dominate the world; their influence is so pervasive and total that whatever problem afflicts them is bound to have far-reaching repercussions throughout the entire fabric of Western Civilization."

In the third century, Tertullian asked, "What has Athens to do with Jerusalem, the Academy with the Church?" Wiser minds than mine have discussed and debated the question for centuries. But I do believe I have something to add to the discussion by way of my experiences at Hope.

None of the issues I encountered at Hope College in the '90s have gone away. They are as disturbingly and dangerously present now, as well as divisive and confounding, as they were then, and even more so. They had to do with the nature of truth, the cult of diversity, the idol of dialogue, the inevitability of the ad hominem argument, and the drift toward violence, presaging what has been called the "cancel culture" today. Most important, they challenged the very content and veracity of orthodox Christian truth, the historic faith "once for all delivered to the saints" (Jude 3 ESV). I'll speak of these in greater detail later.

The experiences I had, and the issues surrounding them, still matter greatly to Christian college administrators, faculties and constituencies, and in some cases the denominations that support them. They certainly matter to the church of Jesus Christ, maybe more so, since most Christian colleges were founded as an outreach of the church. And at the end of the day, what happens in our institutions of higher learning will ultimately matter to our culture, Christian or non-Christian.

The third reason is that the story of the Hope revival is a story of struggle. When I arrived on campus, I asked the college president, John Jacobson, what he thought success would look like in our first year of ministry. He didn't mention numbers, instead he said, "That chapel would matter, that it would be part of the conversation on campus." I was relieved. This thing he called "the Conversation" is a cherished academic value, especially in liberal arts institutions. God willing, chapel ministry would become a part of "the Conversation" at Hope College.

That it did. In spades. I was to learn that "the "Conversation" in a college can have a double edge to it.

No Such Thing as an Immaculate Perception[3]

My reading of the history of campus revivals convinces me that conflict commonly accompanies these awakenings. None of the gains we saw in the '90s came without significant conflict. Not everyone was thrilled with a full chapel, and the spiritual fervor that went with it. Nor were they happy with me, the dean of the chapel. People still argue about the significance and roots of the conflict that emerged during my years at Hope, especially regarding my leadership. I still argue with some of these people, mostly in my mind. In a historical case study of Hope College's Christian identity, authored by two of the Hope faculty, my ministry was described this way:

> With no clear intentions of doing so, Hope College hired one man who in hindsight many would see as transforming the college's religious center of gravity, for good or for ill. Whatever one's judgment

about that, there were very few students, and probably fewer faculty, who did not possess strong feelings about President Jacobson's controversial new Dean of the Chapel . . . feelings strong enough for the campus to erupt in anger and recrimination.[4]

Whew! I've always wanted to make a difference in the world. I like the transformed "religious center of gravity" part. But I didn't have in mind the eruption of "anger and recrimination" that accompanied it. But that's what happened.

Whatever the strengths or weaknesses of what I'm writing about the Hope revival, the conflict section should make for interesting reading. My work at Hope occupies only a little more than a chapter in the book, and I must say the authors were not unfair in the things they said about me. Inaccurate perhaps, but not mean. But the title of the study says a lot about their point of view—*Can Hope Endure*? Did the revival strengthen hope for Hope, or weaken it?

A memoir should be a thoughtful reflection on the past, in this case my past and Hope's past and how the two related. How to write about that part of my past at Hope? How do I perceive it now? I know enough about my own sinfulness and bent toward self-delusion to know "there is no such thing as an immaculate perception." When I write about the conflict at Hope, I don't want to make myself the hero of my own story, or to demonize my opponents. But I may do just that. As I said, this part of the memoir should make for interesting reading. You the reader can decide how well I did. In the end there is only One who fully knows the truth. Amen, Lord. Have mercy on me.

Don't Count the Conflict, Weigh It

It should come as no surprise that a spiritual revival can spark discord. Usually, actually. It goes with the territory. Frederick Buechner said somewhere that childbirth may occasionally be painless, but new birth, never. Revival is hard work, but it's a good hard—like childbirth, or like fighting a good fight, or like running, or like a wrestling match. Metaphors like these abound in the Bible.[5] I love them all. On the one hand it is entirely a gift from God. But on the other hand, as Paul exhorted the Philippians, we must vigorously and strenuously work out what he works in us,[6] and as Jesus said to his disciples, to keep on asking for it, relentlessly.[7] Phillips Brooks's advice on prayer in general applies especially to prayer for revival:

"Do not pray for tasks equal to your powers. Pray for powers equal to your tasks."[8]

Very important: as you read this, do not count the numbers of chapters on revival versus the number of chapters on conflict and struggle, weigh them. If merely counted it might seem that the chapters about the good and the chapters about the bad were equals in the struggle. No way. The reality was and is, the troubles were always "light and momentary." The joy and glory much heavier, in exactly the same way *kabod,* the Hebrew word usually translated "glory" means literally "weight." The revival years at Hope were just as the apostle Paul said of his own work:

For our light and momentary troubles are achieving for us an eternal glory that far outweighs them all. So we fix our eyes not on what is seen, but on what is unseen. For what is seen is temporary, but what is unseen is eternal.
—2 Corinthians 4:17–18

I am grateful that I got to be part of a good fight at Hope College.

Though it became a fight, it started quietly and inauspiciously on a sunny spring morning in 1993, as I walked down Park Avenue in New York City.

2

"Remember When You Thought You Wanted to Work With College Students?"

(From Forest Home's Hormel Hall, 1962, to Hope College's Dimnent Memorial Chapel, 1994)

Unless a kernel of wheat falls to the ground and dies, it remains only a single seed. But if it dies, it produces many seeds.

—John 12:24

I thought it was my voice in my head, just me talking to me, as I walked to a preaching event in midtown Manhattan one day in April 1993. I thought I said to myself, "Remember when you thought you wanted to work with college students?"

The voice and the memory amused me. But later a phone call showed that they were much more than amusement. They were prophecy. They were a summons.

In the moment I just chuckled and mused, "Funny how I thought I wanted to do one thing and ended up doing quite another." I didn't mourn the fact that I didn't end up doing what I had so long wanted to do. I liked what I was doing at age 50, being a pastor to a Presbyterian congregation in New Jersey.

But as I walked I pondered, How long had I thought working with college students would be the perfect job? When did it begin?

A Hot August Night

It began in August 1962, when I was nineteen years old.

It was in the San Bernardino mountains of Southern California, about sixty-five miles east of Los Angeles, at a place called the Forest Home Christian Conference Center. I had come to hear Dr. J. Edwin Orr, an Oxford educated historian, lecture on the history of spiritual awakenings among college students.

Orr was speaking at a conference there called the College Briefing. It was called a "briefing" because it was designed to prepare students to take the gospel of Jesus Christ to their secular campuses. Begun during the Second World War, the "briefing" metaphor was apt and familiar. They were to be "briefed" for spiritual warfare in the same way that soldiers were briefed before going into battle. I knew none of this background when I showed up to hear Orr's lecture. But I was keenly aware of how spiritually hostile my campus was, and how intense the spiritual warfare could be.

Hormel Hall, the venue, was designed, I'm guessing, to comfortably seat four hundred people. There were a lot more than that number crammed into Hormel Hall that evening. It wasn't a "night of fire," as I was to experience at Hope thirty-three years later, but it was a hot August night. And there were a lot of very attractive coeds in the room that frankly were eliciting more interest from me than the speaker I had come to hear. And when Dr. Orr walked onto the platform to speak and I saw what he looked like, his emotional ratings in my callow male psyche dropped even lower. He was a short little man, wearing coke-bottle thick spectacles, a wool tweed coat and a tie. And he spoke with a reedy voice in soft professorial tones. But when he began to tell the stories of God's power to convert and transform colleges, particularly through the prayers of students, I was transfixed—even though he talked for more than ninety minutes.

Vivid in my memory is the story of what is known as the 1806 Haystack Revival at Williams College in Massachusetts. It was so named because the little band of five students who wanted to pray one night was afraid to be seen praying on campus. Hostility toward Christians was so intense that they even kept the minutes of their meetings hidden. So they went off campus to a nearby farm to pray for revival at their school. When a storm broke out, they burrowed under a haystack for protection and kept praying. Their prayers were answered. A spiritual awakening came to Williams College and with it a powerful world missions movement. The youthful leader of that group, Samuel Mills, would later become one of the founders of the American Board of Commissioners for Foreign Missions and the American Bible Society. Today there is a plaque on the site with the inscription: The Birthplace of Foreign Missions.

What impressed me most was that the people Orr talked about were just kids, my age and younger. The hostility I felt on my campus was disguised as yawning indifference, but for them it was deep and nasty. I wondered, if I were to pray, was it possible that God would use me the way he had used the students from Williams College?

Williams College was not unusual for that period, both in its corruption and in its revival. One historian likened college dormitories to "secret nurseries of vice and the cages of unclean birds." At one college, a hole was cut in the center of the college president's Bible, so when he opened it, a deck of playing cards fell out. At another college, a drinking society named itself H.E.O.T.T., a parody of the words of Isaiah 55:1, "Ho, every one that thirsteth" (KJV). And yet, as little bands of students prayed for God to do what only God can do, things changed radically. Schools like Amherst, Dartmouth, Princeton, and Yale saw the conversion of a third to a half of their student bodies. And the changes were not limited to colleges. From top to bottom, American culture and morals were profoundly affected by these awakenings. Again, I hoped and prayed that God would do it again in my day.

What If?

As Orr spoke, my imagination and spiritual longings were fired with a vision of God coming down and transforming a college campus. It would be glorious to be a part of something like those spiritual revivals, I thought. Let it be, I prayed.

There were lots of stops and starts and reversals and renewals over the years since that night, but the vision never completely went away. I was often prone to wander, but God never let me fall away permanently. Throughout the years that followed, there was always a longing, an aching "What if?" in my heart. What if I were allowed to be a part of a sovereign move of the Holy Spirit like the events I had heard about from Dr. Orr?

I remembered how the big "What if?" was nurtured when I started attending First Baptist Church of Pomona the same year I went to the College Briefing Conference. Ted Cole, the pastor of the church, was the first pastor I could identify with. He read books and wrestled with big ideas—some of the same books I was reading and ideas I was wrestling with. He was also an outstanding preacher. I had never met such a man! And through him the door was cracked open in my soul to at least let in the possibility that I, too, might be a pastor one day. It was at First Baptist Church of Pomona that I heard God's call into the ministry.

I remembered the church's vibrant ministry to college students, with two hundred attending a Sunday School class each week. Bill Tipton, the college pastor, was a faithful man with a genius to organize and motivate students. It wasn't long before I eventually got involved. Bill was a man of immense integrity, and a great yet humble mentor. I eventually ended up teaching the Sunday morning class. I loved it.

I remembered that Bill Tipton hired me part time to do an outreach on the Claremont College campuses. It being the '60s, we called the ministry there the New Underground. I guess you had to have been there to see the humor in that moniker. But it was *au courant* for the time. We were to be spiritual subversives, the hidden vanguard, the harbingers of the "Jesus revolution." The '60s, with all their silliness, self-importance, and immorality, were an impossibly optimistic time. I led a Bible study that lasted most of the first year, in the book of Job as I recall. And it was meant to be an outreach to nonbelievers! What were we thinking? I had so much fun. I felt like I had come home. We were so full of ourselves, so immature. But our hearts ached with "What if?" And we prayed earnestly for a spiritual awakening.

The Far Country

I also remembered some bad things: such as the prodigal year I flunked out of seminary. It was the closest I ever came to losing the longing for "What if?"

It had to do with a girl I wanted to marry, but who didn't want to marry me. I was very, very disappointed with God about this. And angry. It took a long time to figure out why, but it eventually became clear to me that deep in the inner recesses of my heart I had signed an agreement with God. Unspoken, of course, unconscious, and unsigned by God. It was this: even though, on one level I knew God owed me nothing whatsoever, I believed on a deeper level that if I lived a good life, he owed me one big thing. That's all, just one. It was her. I had done my part, I had lived a very moral and responsible life. When he didn't deliver on his side of the bargain, I decided it was okay for me to abandon my side too. So I went out and did many things that I was told would ruin my life.

One of those things, but not the worst, was to stop performing academically.

So I was suspended from taking classes for a semester. Before I left, the seminary dean asked if I would sit down for an exit interview. In the course of our conversation, he asked me what I thought I'd like to do, should I ever come back to seminary and graduate. My response was completely unpremeditated. I was surprised at what came out of my mouth. And I promise you that I never forgot the words of my answer. It must have taken all the dean's self-control not to laugh out loud at the answer this failed graduate student gave him.

I'll tell you in a moment what I said.

I Wanted to Be with the Smart People

I remembered one more thing when I heard the voice that day on Park Avenue.

When I finally graduated seminary in 1972, I was a doctrinaire progressive politically, a near socialist. I was still conservative and evangelical theologically, but way out on the left politically. I believed that most of what was wrong with America could probably be traced to some variant of capitalism and to the vague bogey man my friends and I called the "military-industrial complex."[9] Wall Street was to my moral map what Mordor was to the Hobbits.

I was a child of the '60s. With few exceptions, every college and seminary professor I had was a political liberal. Their influence on me was enormous. I blush to admit how much I admired these intellectuals. I was so dazzled by their knowledge and insight, that I uncritically entrusted my naive and eager youth to their wisdom. I wanted to be like them. By the time I graduated seminary, I thought the most fulfilling place to serve the Lord would be among people like them: in a college or university, perhaps, or in a church filled with people like them. I wanted to be with the "smart people." To me the worst, most stultifying place would be to pastor a church filled with businessmen—bankers and entrepreneurs, merchants and other financial types.

Was I really that blinkered and bigoted? Maybe not. But that's how I saw my 1960s and '70s self, as I walked down Park Avenue that spring day in 1994. Here I was in New York City, the belly of the beast I once so loathed. I was going to speak to a large group of business professionals at noon, in an evangelistic outreach called B.O.L.D., an acronym for Business Outreach, Lord Directed. Yikes! And for the last eighteen years I had ministered in churches full of the business kinds of people I once had thought were so one-dimensional and thoughtless.

And I loved it. I loved them.

I found them to be just as smart as the intellectuals I so admired in my sycophant days. Often more so. And creative. And courageous. Unlike many of my professors—not all, but many—their ideas couldn't stay sequestered in the cloister of their heads, untested in the world. Their opinions had to be more than mere theory. They had to be tested against the hard edge of reality, the so-called "bottom line" I once disparaged.

Ray Smith

I was amused and a little embarrassed that day on Park Avenue at what I once thought I had to have to be happy. Nothing had worked out as I had planned, and yet I was a happy man—not in spite of all that, but because of it.

I loved my work and I was in the twenty-first year of a happy, happy marriage to a woman I had never even heard of when I believed God hadn't delivered on his end of the "bargain." As I write this memoir, my wife, Lauretta, and I have been together fifty-two years, and are enjoying our four adult children, their spouses and ten rollicking grandchildren. Significantly, we also met at Forest Home, the summer of 1970. And no, she wasn't in the crowd that night in 1962.

I thanked God that day on Park Avenue for the prayers he didn't grant. And I thought of it no more.

But two weeks later, the phone rang, and my old buddy Ray Smith was on the line.

You need to know who Ray Smith is. I met Ray in 1964, when I joined Forest Home's summer staff two years after the momentous Orr lecture. It was the first of seven summers I worked there, most of which were with the Blue Helmets, a fitness and leadership training program for high school boys.

Ray was my boss that first summer. He had been a football All-American at UCLA, as both a fullback and defensive back. He was captain and most valuable player of the Bruins his senior year. Though fearsome as an athlete, Ray was and is one of the humblest and gentlest men I have ever known. Plus I always laugh a lot when I am with Ray. He was more than a good friend. When I met him in my early twenties, he was the kind of man I hoped to be like when I grew up. Now that I'm grown up, I'm afraid I'm running out of time to be like Ray.

We kept a rigorous regimen with our teenaged charges. Out of bed every morning at five in the morning we ran in the high altitude up to Lake Mears for calisthenics and a "polar bear" swim. After breakfast, we spent the morning doing heavy labor, mainly building rock walls for the conference center. In the afternoon we lifted weights. Evenings we studied the Bible, or listened to some of the speakers Forest Home brought to the center. The sessions lasted five weeks. Interspersed throughout were a camping trip and Dodger and Angels baseball games.

I reveled in all this. From the vantage point of old age, I still look with envy on my young self and marvel that I could eat all I wanted and never gain a pound. I loved the sweat and exertion, the jokes and boisterous male camaraderie.

Ray's significance for this memoir of the Hope Revival is that after that first summer we worked together, he went on to be the head football coach at Hope College. After twenty-five years of coaching, Ray became the winningest football coach in the history of the athletic conference Hope competed in. The Hope College football stadium is named after Ray and his wife, Sue.

It was in that phone call, thirty-one years after we met at Forest Home, that Ray introduced Hope College and Ben Patterson to each other.

After exchanging pleasantries over the phone, Ray said,

"I was at a donut shop last Saturday, and a Hope professor came into the shop and joined me. He was on a committee formed by the college president to help search for the first dean of the chapel at Hope College. They've been at it for weeks, but still haven't found anyone. He asked me if I knew anyone they should look at.

"I said, 'Well, I do know one guy, but I have no idea if he'd be interested.' I told him it was you. He asked me to reach out to you. What do you think, Ben?"

As he said this, I could feel his big, toothy grin on the other end of the line.

Now Is the Time!

I was stunned. I told Ray I'd be interested in exploring the possibility. He said he'd tell the committee I was. And he hung up.

As I sat staring at the telephone, I remembered the voice on Park Avenue. I thought it was my voice. But it was the Holy Spirit who asked me,

"Remember when you thought you wanted to work with college students?"

It was God's voice, no doubt in my mind whatsoever. The timing and juxtaposition of the Park Avenue walk and the phone call from my friend Ray were unmistakable. And even more so in the context of the trajectories of events and experiences in the decades preceding it. The truth was, I had been thinking about working with students for most of my adult life.

Now I can tell you what I said to the dean as I began my disciplinary suspension from seminary. When he asked me what I thought I wanted to do some day, I told him, "I think I'd like to work with college students."

How can I describe what it meant for God to remind me of the very words I had spoken, when the prospects for its fulfillment seemed dead? In my fiftieth year of all times! And to say, now is the time to do what you wanted to do for so long, not then, but now. The fullness of the height and depth God's ways are a mystery to me, but this much is clear: the fact that my prospects died is precisely the reason that this was the right time to embrace them.

It's the gospel way: you find your life by losing it; you die so you can live.

I had to hear God's "no," really take it to heart, with the girl I wanted to marry, and the career I imagined I might pursue, before I could receive his "yes." And God's "yes" is greater than his sternest "no." His "now" is richer and more glorious than his "wait." The woman I eventually married and the family we have raised together far outweigh what I once thought I had lost forever in the bitter years of my disappointment.

"Unless a kernel of wheat falls to the ground and dies, it remains only a single seed. But if it dies, it produces many seeds." (John 12:24)

The dramatic, out-of-the-blue, unanticipated, undeniable sense of God's sovereign call kept me steady in the years of spiritual awakening and conflict that were to follow at Hope. My experience wasn't like Saul on the Damascus road breathing out threats against the Jesus people.

It was just Ben strolling down Park Avenue musing about his life.

But it was real and compelling. It gave me a muscular sense of the certainty of God's call that I would sorely need to stand my ground in the next seven years.

3

"Lord! Make Them Late for Class!"

God explicitly says, "Call unto me , and I will answer." There are no limitations, no hedges, no hindrances in the way of God fulfilling the promise. His word is at stake. God solemnly engages to answer prayer. Man is to look for the answer and be inspired by expectation of the answer. God, who cannot lie, is bound to answer. He has voluntarily placed himself under obligation to answer the prayer of him who truly prays.

—E. M. Bounds

Call unto me, and I will answer thee, and show thee great and mighty things, which thou knowest not.
—Jeremiah 33:3 (KJV)

What shall we say the kingdom of God is like, or what parable shall we use to describe it? It is like a mustard seed, which is the smallest seed you plant in the ground. Yet when planted, it grows and becomes the largest of all garden plants, with such big branches that the birds of the air can perch in its shade.
—Mark 4:30–32

Not to us, O LORD, not to us but to your name be the glory, because of your love and faithfulness.
—Psalm 115:1

About the same time I heard God's voice on Park Avenue in New York, Kim Ebright and a small group of students had been meeting all that year, to pray for revival at Hope. They prayed once a week in a little room outside Hope's dining commons. Jeff Baxter, a senior, formed the group. Kim said that at first she had no idea what he was talking about when he spoke of "spiritual revival." But it gradually came clear when he passed out index cards with little golf pencils and asked her and the other students to write on them the names of professors and students, especially students in fraternities and sororities. They were to pray for them by name, asking God to bring each to a deep and vital faith in Christ.

When Kim found out that I was coming the next year to be Hope's dean of the chapel, she wrote me a letter to welcome me and tell me that she and her friends were praying for revival. She later told me that at the end of the first year they prayed together, they started asking God to make students late for class! Their prayer was, "May there be such a huge crowd in chapel that they'll have a hard time filing out and getting to class on time when chapel is over." That was a crazy prayer for a group that was never more than ten or fifteen students, meeting in a little room outside the dining commons, once a week, between seven and seven thirty in the morning, index cards and golf pencils in hand. How like the God who delights to take weak and foolish things in the world's eyes, to shame the so-called wise and strong.[10]

They weren't the only ones praying. Tim Hamilton, another student, prayed a prayer that made us all smile. Tim had volunteered to run the sound board in our chapel services, that first year. One evening a group of us were praying for the year to come, and we heard him pray, "Lord! Fill the chapel with worshipers this year." Later, some of us on the chapel staff said to each other, "Did you hear what Tim prayed for?" We were touched by his faith, and if truth be told, by his sweet naivete. I worried a little that his young faith might be shaken if his prayer wasn't answered. We even remembered the date he prayed his prayer: July 22, 1994, about a month before we began conducting services in Dimnent Memorial Chapel.

Hope College Students Weren't Interested in Chapel

It wasn't that we didn't believe something like this could happen. We all believed nothing was too hard for God. But we were hedging our prayers. Or tempering them. Maybe someday, after a few years, it would happen at Hope. Maybe. But this would probably take some time, a lot of time. The young usually don't know that. Plus we reminded ourselves that mere numbers don't determine the success of a ministry. The need for a spiritual awakening was obvious, but the prospects for a widespread revival did not look promising.

We looked at the facts, the chief of which was that Hope College students just weren't interested in attending chapel services. Dimnent Memorial Chapel's capacity was twelve hundred, and the handful of students who occasionally attended chapel seemed to roll around in the cold, beautiful sanctuary like a ball bearing in a box car. I even hoped we might be able to start having chapel services in a cozier place, a music department recital room perhaps, and then eventually grow out of it into Dimnent Memorial Chapel.

Where to start? The idea came when I was in Kenya, speaking at a meeting of the Christian Medical and Dental Society. We were driving somewhere, and as I sat in the back seat of the car I saw a strange sight. We were in a region dotted with several large ant-hill shaped hills, each hill covered by little villages, each distinctively separate from the others, close, but apart. The thought came to me: *that's Hope College, spiritually. There are a lot of little Christian groups there that don't have much to do with each other. You need to gather these separate Christian villages into one big town.* The thought—or was it the voice I heard earlier that year on Park Avenue?—seemed different from my usual musings. But I didn't spend any time wondering where it came from. It just seemed like a good idea.

When I got back from the trip I told my newly formed Campus Ministries staff what I saw. It was March 1994, six months before we formally began our ministry in September. We were very much in the planning stage of the year ahead. We agreed that a big part of our strategy for spiritual revival at Hope would be to gather together its scattered "villages" of Christian groups. That's how we came up with the name for Hope's celebrated Sunday evening meeting, The Gathering.[11]

Where to start The Gathering? Which "village"? As we prayed, the obvious place to start was where the spiritual energy was in the Hope community. We reasoned, that since God is always ahead of us, always the initiator, we should find out where he is already at work and jump on board.

It wasn't hard to see where the vibrancy was. It was clearly with students who were a part of the Lakeshore Vineyard Church in Holland. The pastor, Paul Bradford, and I became close friends in the years ahead, but at the time all I knew about his church was that it was heavily influenced by charismatic renewal. That is to say, the students there were eager for pure experience, to encounter God in all the "charisms," the manifestations of the Holy Spirit mentioned in the New Testament, including the more "ecstatic" manifestations—everything from healings and dreams and visions, to speaking in tongues and being "slain" in the Spirit.

Their Zeal Was Compelling

Had I come to Hope College even six months earlier, all that would have made me extremely uncomfortable. I hadn't dismissed it as unbiblical, it just gave me the creeps. I was a Calvinistic Presbyterian. I was nurtured on prayer and sound Bible exposition. I thrived on the life of the mind. The people I knew who were into all those manifestations often struck me as immature and hysterical. To be honest, I was a little prejudiced emotionally toward those who spoke in so-called "tongues," glossolalia, or unknown prayer languages. To be honest, I was also probably jealous of the intimacy they seemed to have with God. But something had happened to me that changed that profoundly. I describe it in chapter ten, "Something Like a Language."

The spiritual energy of what the Lord was doing with these precious students animated our chapel services. We never tried to replicate the way things happened in the Vineyard, but the warmth and exuberance of the Vineyard kids energized everything we did. Their zeal was magnetic—it helped to gather many other students to worship the true and living God. The prophetic vision I saw in the little villages on the hills in Kenya, gradually became one grand movement of the Holy Spirit at Hope College.

Kim Ebright and Tim Hamilton were involved in the Lakeshore Vineyard Church.

We decided to start small, programmatically. We wanted to find an attainable entry point for students who might be skeptical or jaded about chapel. Hoping to convince the student body that chapel wasn't going to be a dreary affair, we held our first two services outdoors. Monday evening of the August orientation week we had the service in a copse of trees known as the Pine Grove. We advertised it as—ta da!—"Groovin' in the Grove." It was very, very basic: mainly a goofy skit and some singing. It was fun, and it went well. Again, on Thursday morning, we held our second chapel service in the Pine Grove. More of the same. Then on Friday morning, when we invited the students to come indoors in Dimnent Memorial Chapel for the first time, they came in by the hundreds. Before long, we were averaging over five hundred in attendance. Chapel attendance was an instant sensation in Holland, Michigan. The local newspaper even ran a front-page story about students packing Dimnent Memorial Chapel. Just about everybody at the college was happy, especially the students.

But not everybody. More on that in later chapters.

They Were Asking the Wrong Questions

Over the years, Hope College had acquired a bad reputation among area churches for spiritual life on campus. Dismal chapel attendance was perceived as just another symptom of a general spiritual malaise on campus. Although no longer formally connected to the Reformed Church in America, the ties remained emotionally strong between the two entities. Justifiably pleased and proud of such a big spike in chapel attendance, President Jacobson even invited pastors of churches in the region to come to a chapel service, have lunch afterward and meet for a question and answer session with some students and the chapel staff.

A lot of pastors came, and everyone seemed to have a good time. After chapel and lunch we gathered in the balcony of Dimnent Memorial Chapel for Q and A. I was disappointed at the things they wanted to talk about. After all we had said to them about the supernatural work of God at Hope, the questions they kept asking us were anything but supernatural. They were entirely about programs and techniques. What kind of music do students like? What are the topics you speak on?

I could see Kim Ebright, fidgeting in the corner. She raised her hand, and asked to speak.

I wish you could have seen and heard this lovely young college junior rebuke her elders. And the thing was, she did it so graciously and earnestly that it didn't feel like a rebuke. But it was. She said, "It's not about the music and program. It's about God showing his power. What you are seeing is what happens when God answers prayer."

She had caught the vision of what so moved me many years before when I was a student hearing a lecture on students, prayer and spiritual awakenings in American history. Revival does not come from applying a technique, but from God sovereignly acting in response to his people's prayers. How this all works, how his sovereign will and our human freedom interact in the spiritual realm, I didn't know then and I don't know now. But it seems clear in the Bible and in history that a God who can do anything he chooses, chooses not to do some things until we ask, even plead. Even our desires and askings come from God. All our prayers are answers to God's "prayer" that we pray.[12] What I first heard from J. Edwin Orr in 1962, I believed and still believe: that whenever God wants to do something, he sets his people to praying.[13]

This doesn't mean that good programs and relevant music and skilled staff don't matter. They do. Indeed, Max and Connie Boersma had generously endowed the college with a financial gift that enabled us to do all those things and more. But it's a huge mistake to confuse the means God provides with God himself. It's idolatry. "Unless the LORD builds the house, its builders labor in vain" (Psalm 127:1). What we saw God do at Hope was more than the sum of its parts and people.

In the years ahead, chapel attendance swelled to standing room only, every time the doors to Dimnent Memorial Chapel were opened. Bible study groups and student mission outreaches multiplied. The first year we announced sign-ups for spring mission trips, some students spent the night outside the office to make sure they got a space. Hope College had not seen enthusiasm like this since the days of the Student Volunteer movement a century before.

"This Is the Holy Spirit, Call Me!"

Dwight Beal, our worship leader, was key. He put together a "worship team" of students to help him lead singing in the chapel services with guitar, voice, and drums. The singing was followed by a short message from the Bible, usually evangelistic, or something about Christian living. We blush to remember the music. Dwight and his friend John Grooters had been leading worship at Christian youth camps all summer. Dwight remembers,

> We'd been playing from camp to camp and pretty much all of our chapel songs had hand motions. We had no drums, so I programmed all the drums into my Korg keyboard.

The students who were coming to chapel may have been versed in the riches of traditional church music. But the simplicity of the songs in Dwight's repertoire seemed exactly appropriate for where many students were musically and spiritually.

The music and mood in chapel ranged from boisterous and uproarious to reverent silence, often in the same service. Students would sing their hearts out one moment, and in an instant lean forward to hear the Word of God preached. We met for twenty-two minutes each Monday, Wednesday, and Friday, and for ninety minutes on Sunday evenings in The Gathering. We were amazed at how rich those little twenty-two minute services were. The time was short, but so much seemed to happen in them that we often felt we had been lingering leisurely at the feet of Jesus. The Sunday evening Gathering, the longer meeting, soon became the centerpiece of the chapel ministry, and the place where so much of the spiritual awakening took place.

Holy Hilarity

My first conversation with Dwight Beal was memorable and significant. It's sweet to look back from the vantage point of all that's happened at Hope since, and see how the Holy Spirit was already setting trajectories for the years to come.

Dwight was a fairly recent Hope graduate. I first heard about him because of his reputation as a musician and worship leader. I needed someone to help us with music in the chapel ministry, so I called, left a voicemail, and waited for him to answer the call.

He didn't.

I'll let Dwight pick up the story from here.

> I got home after a weekend away, and there was a message on my answering machine. The voice said, "Dwight, this is Ben Patterson and I'm here to start a new thing at Hope College, and I'd just love to talk to you about it."
>
> I ignored the call. I thought, oh, whatever. I'm still paying off my student loans. I don't need to talk to this guy about Hope College. He called me again and left a second message. I didn't get back to him the second time either.
>
> And then he called and left a third voicemail. He laughingly said, "Dwight, this is the Holy Spirit, call me!" So I decided that whoever this cat is, I've got to call him back. I did and we decided to meet in the Kletz, the college coffee shop.
>
> Ben asked me how he could recognize me when he saw me. I told him I looked like a hippie. So I asked him how I could recognize him, and he said, "I'm devastatingly handsome."

In that exchange, a relationship trajectory was set: a playful, prayerful and gentle mirthfulness that permeated the whole chapel staff for the next seven years. I had never met this guy, and here I was, already joking around with him and he with me. Things were going to get terribly serious and difficult in the future, but we could always laugh and clown around. Always.

In the staff that emerged in those first years, everybody thought everybody else was funny.

There was my secretary Dani Hadley—earnest in prayer and love for Jesus, whose wisecracks and East Coast bluntness (she was a New Jersey native) kept us all a little off-balance, and whose reenactments of skits she saw on Saturday Night Live were funnier than the skits themselves.

There was Paul Boersma—a man who breathed friendliness, whose eyes moistened when we sang "Amazing Grace," a quintessential Dutchman with no guile, always ready for a round of golf or a basketball game, pizza and a Mountain Dew, or to talk trash about any sports team playing his team. He was also a man of prayer and a lover of Christ and the gospel.

And there was Dolores Nasrallah—like me an émigré from California, a natural counselor whose very being invited people to open their hearts to her, and whose infectious, rollicking laugh would fill the room, even when we were laughing at the "creative" ways the people in Holland misspelled her name. She was another wise and earnest disciple and woman of prayer.

A couple of years into our time together, Cheri Beals joined the staff as an administrative assistant. Cheri's quiet and gracious steadiness and authority was much needed. Whenever I started to get a little too boisterous in my levity, Cheri helped me stay on track, not as a guardrail, but as loving leaven, serious with a dazzling smile. She was artistic and organized, and another person of earnest prayer.

Over the years the composition of the chapel staff would change and grow in numbers, but the rare combination of deep piety and holy hilarity remained, a gift from God, especially when times were tough.

God Meant to Overanswer an Audacious Prayer

It used to worry me that I am such a sucker for a laugh and people who make me laugh. There were probably times in my raw youth, when people I found funny led me into sin—well no, not probably but definitely did lead me into sin. But somewhere along the way, the Lord baptized my fondness for humor and silliness and made it a source of strength and perseverance in the hard times at Hope. I was reassured to learn that the martyr and saint Sir Thomas More, was known for his sense of humor. He even kept a monkey and a resident comedian in his home. More prayed, "Lord, give me a sense of humor, and I will find happiness in life and profit for others." More had his monkey and his comedian. I had something better: a prayerful and merry staff.

Remembering our first conversation in the college coffee shop, Dwight said:

> We found each other with no problem, and after a few moments of effortless frivolity, Ben leaned forward and said to me, as serious

he could be, "Dwight, I'm convinced that if we can gather even a small core of worshipers, the ends of the earth will feel the impact."

I was intrigued to say the least. But what Ben was saying and what I knew of the cultural climate at Hope College did not seem to fit together. So I asked him, "Ben . . . how in the world did you get here?" He said very matter-of-factly, "God called me." And after mulling this conversation over in my mind for the next month, I sensed God calling me too.

The students had prayed an audacious prayer: that God would fill the chapel with worshipers. God meant to "overanswer" that prayer, because his ultimate intent has always been to fill the whole world with worshipers, not just Dimnent Memorial Chapel. What would happen at Hope would impact the world.

God's purposes are mysterious, from everlasting to everlasting, and always solely at his initiative. "Who has known the mind of the Lord? Or who has been his counselor?" (Romans 11:34). In that first year, our first glimpses of his grand intentions for Hope College were in seeds sown quietly in little prayer groups, the joyous fellowship of friends, exuberant chapel worship and the preaching of God's Word.[14]

At the end of that first golden year we were so grateful and satisfied with the success we experienced, we were tempted to think we had seen it all. But we would have been wrong. God had much more in mind than a vibrant, well-attended chapel ministry for Hope College.

He always has.

4
Nights of Fire[15]

I pray that you, being rooted and established in love, may have power . . .
to grasp how wide and long and high and deep is the love of Christ.
                                        —Ephesians 3:17–18

Question 1. What is your only comfort in life and in death?
That I am not my own but belong—body and soul, in life and in death—to
my faithful Savior, Jesus Christ.

Question 2. What must you know to live and die in the joy of this comfort?
Three things: first, how great my sin and misery are; second, how I am set
free from all my sins and misery; third, how I am to thank God for such
deliverance.

                                        —The Heidelberg Catechism

Fancy upsetting the clock-like, mechanical perfection of a great service
with an outpouring of the Spirit. The thing is unthinkable!

                                        —Martyn Lloyd-Jones

Then came that unforgettable week—April 9–16, 1995—the nights
of fire.
It started at The Gathering, in Dimnent Memorial Chapel, at one
of the last worship services of the 1994–95 academic year.

My first year as dean of the chapel at Hope College was about to con-
clude jubilantly, with a bang, not the whimper that often pervades the spring
semester in colleges. It had been a good year, a great year! And I was feeling
good. A decades-long decline in chapel attendance was reversed, and students were coming to chapel services in record numbers. The energy around
the chapel ministry was infectious. Chapel at Hope College was definitely
part of the conversation on campus. My staff and I hoped things would pick
up in the fall where they had left off in the spring. We were grinning and
grateful and relaxed, a little loose, high-fiving each other at our last staff
meeting. We were very thankful.

Two Fears

But I was afraid of two things that night at The Gathering.

My first fear was that my invitation would be met with silence. I had invited the students gathered in Dimnent Memorial Chapel to respond at the microphone to the testimonies they heard from the guest speakers that evening, three students from Wheaton College. Three microphones were set up on the chapel floor for that purpose. It is an understatement to say the Wheaton students' witness was unusual.

What if the students didn't respond at all? The silence would be awkward.

My second fear was slightly worse: what if they *did* respond? It could be messy, and hugely controversial. So I probably went overboard with disclaimers—"I don't want to manipulate . . . engineer an event . . . make anything happen. . . . You may leave now if you want . . . etc." Then I walked off the platform down the stairs to the chapel floor, with the intent of moderating whatever happened at the mics. I was almost afraid to look out to see if any students were approaching the front to speak.

Immediately, scores of college students lined up on both sides of the chapel, waiting for a chance to stand before a microphone to publicly confess their sins and tell of their personal burdens. That's right, publicly. I was amazed. I had heard about events like this before in American history, and had wondered what it would be like. I was about to find out.

The confessing and sharing began around nine o'clock and continued until three in the morning! And again, the next night and the next, into the wee hours of the morning each time. Hundreds of students publicly opened up their lives to each other and the Lord as they confessed gossip, spiritual laziness, cheating, sexual immorality, rape, incest, abortion, eating disorders, alcohol abuse, broken relationships, struggles with pornography and anxiety and alcohol abuse, and on and on and on; all out loud and before an audience. The only sin or struggle I didn't hear confessed was murder.

Divine Choreography

After the first student spoke I worried about what would happen next. What should I do? What could I do? He had actually confessed the sin of incest. Would he just walk away alone and untended? Should I be ready to jump up and put my arm around him and pray for him?

No need. He was immediately surrounded by friends who did all those things. This happened over and over again, with no exceptions, like a divinely ordered choreography, orderly and quietly. Surprising to me, but not to anyone familiar with revival, the meetings were peppered with tears and smiles, laughter and singing. Although the pain in many lives was palpable, more poignant was the way after each and every student spoke, he or she would be gently "mobbed" by friends—hugging, praying, encouraging, and assuring them of God's love and forgiveness as well as their own. Several times, students who were sitting in the back of the chapel, were so anxious to pray for a friend who had just confessed, they would walk down to the front on the backs of the pews, like they were stilts. It was delightfully noisy.

What prompted the students to do this? I have a short answer and a longer answer. The short answer is that the Holy Spirit did it. No question about this. No slick program ploy or charismatic speaker can motivate students to do what they were doing. The question is not *what*, but *Who* prompted the event. It was him. It was the third member of the Trinity.

The longer answer is the means the Spirit often uses to do his work. For some time, there had been a growing sense of expectancy on campus, that God was going to do extraordinary things—in fact he was already doing them at Hope. Many prayers had been offered up for him to send a spiritual awakening to a college that had been slipping from its Christian moorings for many years. There were also the testimonies that night, the words of witness from the Wheaton guests. God, it seems, loves to use the simple personal witness of simple believers, anointed by his Spirit to change lives.

Our visiting guests had come to testify about the extraordinary things they experienced on their campus, three weeks before, beginning Sunday, March 19. A Hope College student was with them, since she had been at Wheaton visiting a friend and had attended the meetings.

This was their testimony: Students from Howard Payne University in Texas came to Wheaton to give witness to a recent spiritual revival on their campus, which had been characterized by public confession and repentance of sin. After their presentation, microphones were opened up for Wheaton students to respond to what they heard. What happened at Howard Payne, then happened at Wheaton, and went on for three days. Now it was happening at Hope.

Actually, I learned later it was happening at many other places too, over roughly the same time frame; Moody Bible Institute, Chicago, Illinois; Messiah College, Grantham, Pennsylvania; Columbia University, New York City; Trinity Christian College, Palos Heights, Illinois; Northwestern College, St. Paul, Minnesota; Asbury University, Wilmore, Kentucky; Trinity International University, Deerfield, Illinois; Gordon College, Wenham, Massachusetts; Eastern Nazarene College, Quincy, Massachusetts; Cornerstone University, Grand Rapids, Michigan; Taylor University, Upland, Indiana; Iowa State University, Ames, Iowa; George Fox College, Newburg, Oregon; Multnomah School of the Bible, Portland, Oregon; Judson College, Elgin, Illinois; Yale University, New Haven, Connecticut; University of Wisconsin, Steven's Point, Wisconsin.[16]

Accounts of these and other happenings appeared in publications as diverse as *Christianity Today, New York Times* and *Chronicle of Higher Education*. As I write this account in 2023, a similar revival has happened again at Asbury University, in Wilmore, Kentucky.[17]

As I listened, I was touched by the simple, unaffected authenticity and power of what they had experienced. One of the Wheaton students began his testimony saying, "I'm not much of a public speaker," and then went on to show that he wasn't. But his lack of skill made the story he told of God's work in his life even more credible.

Messy and Raw Like Surgery

This event was much more than the sum of its parts; it was a powerful work of the Holy Spirit—simple testimony shared quietly, without any hype. Sins were confessed, for heaven's sake! Publicly! It's hard enough for most of us to admit our sins to ourselves or to a trusted friend. But in a room of hundreds, mostly strangers and perhaps a few friends? This kind of thing goes way beyond emotional exhibitionism. Mere regrets for moral lapses do not produce public confession. Only deep repentance does. When David Thoreau neared death, he was asked if he intended to make his peace with God. He replied, "I didn't know we had quarreled." It was obvious these students knew they had quarreled with God, and that this demanded heartfelt repentance and confession. And all the while, the body of Christ, though young and in many ways immature and unseasoned, acted like the body of Christ, receiving, forgiving and encouraging fellow sinners.

It was messy and sometimes raw as I had feared. Of course it was. Surgery is messy. Just think of the sins that were publicly confessed.

And it was controversial and misunderstood as I also feared. The Anchor, Hope's student newspaper, later reported it as an innovative program the chaplain's staff had dreamed up that "was so successful the chaplains decided to do it another night." My staff and I chuckled over that one;

imagining a brainstorming session for innovative program initiatives where someone said, "Hey! I have a great idea! Let's ask the students to share their deepest, darkest personal secrets in public. We can advertise it the week before in chapel."

More serious were angry accusations of spiritual abuse and pastoral malpractice in a long letter to the editor of the student newspaper, by an ad hoc group calling itself C.A.R.E., an acronym for Concerned about Responsible Education. The volume went up in the rumblings and grumblings that had been going on all year in certain sectors of the faculty, as the chapel services grew in strength and energy.

I sympathized with the accusers. Most, if not all of them, had not been there. I might have reacted in the same way, if I hadn't been there and had only heard of it. It did sound bizarre. But what I witnessed and experienced was not bizarre. It was healing. It was messy in the most orderly way, like surgery. At times, it even seemed like a kind of liturgy, in the way confession and repentance and restoration were enacted in those services.

My emotions surprised me during the meetings. I was so absorbed in maintaining proper decorum and "shepherding" the confessions that I felt excessively sober and matter of fact about the raw things I heard. Most of the time I was so preoccupied with shepherding, that I felt like a sheep dog scampering around the edges of the flock. But when I went home and went to bed during those three "nights of fire," I would wake up in the night, quietly weeping over what I heard: so many wrenching confessions of the pain these students had received, and the pain they had given—a generation ravaged by Satan, sacrificed to Molech,[18] but loved by Jesus who came to seek and to save the lost. To think that Christ bore all that in his body on the cross! Good Friday, which came later in the week, was never so meaningful.

Deeper than the Cerebral Cortex

One student's story still stands out to me. In the meetings, she spoke of the Spirit's conviction that she be reconciled to her father. When I was able to talk to her about it later, she told me that years before he had abandoned her mother and her sisters, for another, younger woman—his secretary, no less. She hated him for his infidelity, more so perhaps because of its shabbiness, and she hadn't spoken to him since. When I asked her how her efforts toward reconciliation were going, she described the awkwardly painful bumblings I had seen so many times in my years as a pastor. No quick fix here, just very human attempts to do the right thing in the power of the Holy Spirit. It would be a long road, but it started that night. Stories like this abounded among the students.

I had been at Hope College for more than a year, and thought I had a pretty good idea of where the students were emotionally and spiritually. But in many ways the week of the "nights of fire" was a reintroduction, opening my eyes to deeper insights into both their hurts and their longings.

It became clearer than ever that they hungered for an experience of God—one in which the church and confession and forgiveness went deeper than the cerebral cortex. They weren't looking for a faith that went against reason; they wanted a faith that took them further than mere reason can. They wanted the something that Pascal understood when he wrote, "The heart has reasons which reason does not know." They wanted to experience the gospel—concretely, physically, emotionally, incarnationally, in their flesh and blood.

The confessions meant they could know and be known to each other, warts and all, and be loved nevertheless. These students had been lied to. In one way or another they had been taught to believe that they were alone in their struggles, and therefore isolated from not only the body of Christ, but the rest of humanity. Though sometimes immature and awkward and discomfiting, the awakening was a powerful rebuttal of that lie. Being fully known by Christ and more fully known to each other went hand in hand.

This fact alone would account for the significance of the "nights of fire." Some of the student's confessions, things like attempted suicide and eating disorders, placed them in what some would term the "at risk" category, and indicate the need for medical attention. Actually, as we discovered later, some of them were already in psychotherapy and had been for some time. A critic of the revival asked me why I didn't stop the meetings when I saw the direction it was heading—full public disclosure and all that. Besides confessing that I believed it was a work of God, all I could say was that I wasn't going to cut off the sharing, but affirm their legitimate hunger to be known, and to walk with them in it.

It takes a large measure of discernment and humility to be an effective pastor in events like these. Were some students confessing more out of narcissism than genuine repentance? Probably. Which ones? I don't know. Will some of the things that were brought out into the open eventually be used against the students? Perhaps. I don't know of any. Were some of the students immature and intemperate in their claims about the supernatural nature of the "nights of fire"? Yes, I think so. Maybe. Have some fallen back into bad attitudes and behavior? Certainly. All of the above.

But Jesus said the kingdom is like that: a mixture of wheat and weeds, of true and false, and that we should not be so eager to pull the weeds that we destroy the wheat in the process.[19] The good is often tinged with ambiguity in this world.

Jesus also said the Spirit is like the wind, not to be controlled. Sometimes when the Spirit blows through the church, our little mechanisms of control get blown away, or bypassed altogether.

My experience of the revival at Hope highlighted forcibly the importance of the trust and humility required to let go of the control of everything that happens in my ministry. The weakness of the church, at least in much of the global West, suggests what we need now is not restraint but arousal and awakening. That can make for messiness and confusion. But better the messiness of life than the predictability of rigor mortis.

Baptized in Tears

Shortly after the "nights of fire" I heard a Methodist minister from Texas tell of what happened to him when he baptized the leader of the local Latin Kings gang. The young man had come to faith in Christ just days before. The pastor described his view of the boy's broken nose as he lowered him into the water, and then of the youth shaking and sobbing when he was brought up out of the water. Later the boy told him that this was only the second time in his life he had cried. The first time was when he was seven and his father struck him with his fist and broke his nose. Then the pastor told us, "I baptized him with water, but he baptized me with his tears—and they washed away a lot of church stuff."

I knew a little of what that pastor experienced as I sat through the nights of fire. It is true—when the Spirit comes with power, unnecessary accretions of "church stuff" get washed away.

The timing of the revival meetings was significant. They began the first day of Holy Week, the evening of Palm Sunday, and for two more nights. Then students went home for Easter break. They came back for a final evening of thanksgiving the evening of Resurrection Sunday. It struck me that all this had happened in the context of the remembrance of Christ's sufferings and resurrection. The gospel was enacted, and the great creeds illustrated: Christ came, Christ died for our sins, and was raised for our justification.

Glory and Contentiousness

Looking back, I think the location of the revival meetings was significant too. They began in the college, but concluded in a church building across the street from the campus, at Pillar Reformed Church, because Dimnent Memorial Chapel had been booked by another group that evening. That was as it should be; God's mercy at Hope College was not just for college students but for his whole church and the whole world. As I write this, Jonathon Brown, the pastor of Pillar Reformed Church, was a student who was later touched by the revival.

For the many who attended those meetings in April 1995 there was a deep sense that God had visited Hope College in a powerful and defining way. Things had been changing all year—but after those nights, they *changed*. Before those nights in April we hoped that things would pick up in the fall where they left off in the spring. But things went beyond where they had left. The first year attendance in Chapel was a few hundred. The next year it was standing room only, as depicted in the Schoon-Tanis painting—the aisles of Dimnent crammed with standing students, every time its doors were opened.

And there was even more coming.

5

"That's Not A Big Enough Job"

The Church exists by mission, just as a fire exists by burning.
—Emil Brunner

The evangelization of the world in this generation.
—the rallying cry of the Student Volunteer
movement, ca. 1886

Their challenge to other students was not, "Pray for me," or
"Please support me," but rather, "Come with me."
—Steve Shadrach

God helping me, I propose to be a foreign missionary.
—a decision card signed by college
senior Samuel Zwemer, ca. 1887

D wight, I'm convinced that if we can just gather a small core of worshipers, I know the ends of the earth will feel the impact."
Did I say that?

I don't remember saying it, but Dwight Beal said I said it in our first
meeting in the Kletz. When he told me about it, I thought, that's a pretty
good quote. It's nice to hear myself quoted and not be embarrassed.

The Greater Significance

I really believed every word of what I didn't remember saying. I had
been convinced for some time that the greater significance of the Hope
chapel ministry, particularly its worship, would mean that the ends of the
earth would feel the impact of the worship of the triune God at Hope
College. I was honestly surprised that after little more than a year of ministry, Dimnent Memorial Chapel was packed, standing room only, every
time its doors were opened. I was delighted too. Christ was being exalted,
students' lives were being changed, and the college's descent into theolog-

ical heterodoxy was being stanched somewhat, or at least challenged. But I'll say it again: the greater significance of all those good things would be much more than a robust chapel program. The greater significance of the revival would be the effect the worship of God at Hope College would have on the peoples of the earth.

Nothing new here, really. This was the very reason Hope College was founded. The dissident Dutch settlers who settled in West Michigan, mid-nineteenth century, wanted to establish a college that would train people to teach school and take the gospel to the ends of the earth. I knew very little about this before I began my duties as a dean at the college.

There was nothing new here for me either. Long before I knew there was such a thing as Hope College, I believed it was the calling of every Christian in Christ's church to make disciples of all peoples. Throughout high school and college I was taught that there is an indissoluble connection between worship and this glorious mission. Later, as a pastor, I read John Piper's 1993 book, *Let the Nations Be Glad*. No one has said this better than Piper:

> Missions is not the ultimate goal of the church. Worship is. Missions exist because worship doesn't. Worship is the ultimate, not missions, because God is ultimate, not man. . . . [Worship] is the fuel and goal of missions. . . . Passion for God in worship precedes the offer of God in preaching. You can't commend what you don't cherish. Missionaries will never call out, "Let the nations *be glad!*" if they cannot say from the heart, "I *rejoice* in the LORD. . . . *I will be glad and exult in you*, I will sing praise to your name, O Most High" (Pss. 104:34; 9:2). Missions begins and ends in worship.[20]

This was solidified in a prophetic charge I was given when the good people of my last pastorate, the Presbyterian Church in New Providence, New Jersey, sent me off to Hope College. It was both a goodbye and a charge to missions. One of the church members, David Bryant, a great man of prayer, delivered the charge. It came principally from Isaiah 49:6, and it sang in my heart as though it were written for me personally.

> He says, "But that's not a big enough job for my servant—
> just to recover the tribes of Jacob,
> merely to round up the strays of Israel.
> I'm setting you up as a light for the *nations*
> so that my salvation becomes *global!*" (The Message)

That line, "But that's not a big enough job for my servant— just to recover the tribes of Jacob, merely to round up the strays of Israel," drilled me. I knew the chapel program at the college was gasping, virtually on life support. I felt the pressure to renew it. I wanted to succeed. But what if I did succeed? What if my work even became a stunning success? I heard the Holy Spirit say to me, "Ben, that would be too small a thing. Your thinking is too small. I want something bigger for Hope. I want to make what happens at Hope College to be a light to the peoples of the earth, 'so that my salvation becomes global!'"

Let me be emphatic and clear. The servant of the Lord in this passage is none other than Jesus the Messiah, not Ben Patterson, dean of the chapel. But as a servant of the servant, I share in his mission, as all believers do. To my surprise that evening, as I heard the charge for my work at Hope, it began to dawn on me, with fear and trembling, that I was getting involved in something far larger and weightier than I had imagined. I hadn't a clue as to how it would come about, but I was beginning to understand that my greatest desires for my work at Hope were "not a big enough job." That was way too small. I was hearing much more than a charge that night, I was hearing a prophecy.

A Dream

Now for some this may start sounding a little weird. There was another reason I believed in this "greater significance" of the worship at Hope College, and it wasn't theological, per se. It was that I had a dream about it. Yes, a dream, the kind of thing you have when you're sleeping. I've only had a handful of dreams like this in my life, in which I was sure the dream came from God. This was one of them. How do I know when a dream comes from God? I just know that I know that I know when it happens,

The dream came one night as my family and I were camping at one of my favorite places on earth, the Grand Canyon. We were on the north rim of the canyon, the summer of 1994, just before I began conducting chapel services at Hope. In the dream I was having a conversation with a man I knew who was very wealthy and influential in the world. He was a real person, but his name isn't important for this narrative. He was offering me an opportunity to travel globally and preach the gospel to peoples all over the planet. He would set it up and fund it. As exciting and appealing as that was, I was politely declining his offer. I wanted to do it, but there was no way I could or should.

I said to him, "Now isn't the time for something like this. I'm about to begin a new work at Hope College. My wife and I have four children, and it would be criminal to her and the kids for me to be off traveling all the time, not to mention unethical when I have major responsibilities at the college."

He kept gently prodding me to consider his offer, smiling in such a way that seemed to me in my dream to be hopeful. This went on for a while, him offering, me declining.

Then I looked to my left, and I saw that my wife, Lauretta, had been sitting there all the while. And I saw that she was nodding in agreement with the man who was making the offer. She was saying yes, it would be okay for me to do this thing.

I began to weep with joy when I saw her agreement.

Then suddenly the scene changed. As happens only in dreams, I was standing with her on the lawn outside Dimnent Memorial Chapel. It was dark outside, and the stained glass windows in the chapel were beaming with light. We could hear music coming from inside, so we walked over to the doors of Dimnent and opened them. The scene was glorious. The chapel was full of students singing exuberantly, and there was a black gospel choir singing up front. In the middle of it all was Paul Boersma, one of the chaplains on my staff, doing what he always does, grinning and having fun, meeting and greeting people, shaking hands and taking care of business.

We stepped away from the scene and looked around the campus. Though silent, the message was commandingly clear. God said, "You won't have to travel the globe to preach the gospel. It will go out from here."

Then I woke up into a gray dawn on the edge of the Grand Canyon, just before sunup. And I knew that I knew that I knew the significance of what was going to happen at Hope.

What I didn't know was how anchored in Hope's founding mission my dream was, and how savage the battle would be to restore it. The battle was more than hinted at in the other Scripture David Bryant read to me in his charge. It was from God's call to Jeremiah—

Get up and prepare for action.
Go out and tell them everything I tell you to say.
Do not be afraid of them,
or I will make you look foolish in front of them.
For see, today I have made you strong
like a fortified city that cannot be captured,
like an iron pillar or a bronze wall.

You will stand against the whole land—
the kings, officials, priests, and people of Judah.
They will fight you, but they will fail.
For I am with you, and I will take care of you.
I, the LORD, have spoken!
                                    —Jeremiah 1:17–19 NLT

I'll say more about that later.

"God helping me, I propose to be a foreign missionary."

Soon after I arrived at Hope, I learned of two young men, both students, who emerged early in Hope's history, and whose lives embodied both Hope's mission and the struggle to maintain it.

The first was a visitor from Princeton Seminary, who was invited to speak to the student body sometime in the academic year, 1886–87. He immediately got the students' attention with a map of India and a metronome set on a table in front of it. As it ticked off the seconds, he invited the Hope College[21] students in the audience to imagine each click to be the life of someone in that great subcontinent who had just died without knowing Jesus Christ and his gospel. As the metronome quietly ticked away, and the young man spoke, Hope students were riveted by his passion for the gospel, and the enormity of so many lives facing eternity without Christ.

His name was Robert Wilder. He and another Princeton student were spending the year traveling and speaking to students in 162 colleges across the East Coast and Midwest. Their mission was singular: it was an appeal for college students to consider joining them to take the gospel to the unevangelized peoples of the earth. They were part of a larger group of one hundred students who had committed themselves to this mission the summer before in 1886, after attending the first student Bible conference in American history in Northfield, Massachusetts. They came to call themselves the Student Volunteer movement. Their slogan was, "The evangelization of the world in this generation." Over the next forty years, more than twenty thousand students answered that call, going to the myriad parts of the world where there was no gospel witness.

Wilder couldn't have made his appeal in a more receptive place than Hope College. Essentially, he was recruiting students in a college and a community that was founded to do the very thing he was recruiting them to do. They had volunteered before they volunteered.

Among the students listening to Wilder was the second young man, Samuel Zwemer, a twenty-year-old senior from Vriesland, Michigan. Born April 12, 1867, Zwemer was the thirteenth of fifteen children born to Dutch Separatist immigrants, who had sailed to America, just eighteen years before, in 1849. Persecuted in their native land for their evangelical faith and missionary zeal, they came to Michigan to establish a community where they could practice their evangelical faith and send missionary evangelists to the ends of the earth. They came amid terrible hardships—death, disease and famine. On the voyage across the Atlantic alone, seven of the 178 passengers on the ship Leyla died, all children. But nevertheless, they had no sooner landed in Michigan than they began to make plans to build a college to educate men and women for service, especially missions. As early as 1851, though they lived barely above the poverty level, the settlers committed themselves to setting aside 15 percent of church money for foreign missions, and 50 percent for home missions. This was just two years after they arrived! Amazingly, fifteen years later, on June 24, 1864, they laid the keel for a boat they intended to sail from Lake Michigan through the inland waterways to the Atlantic Ocean to take the gospel to the nations.

To use a modern idiom, missions and education were in Hope's spiritual DNA.

When Wilder finished his appeal before the students that day in 1887, he challenged them to sign a card, and pledge themselves to global missions. Breathlessly, with the metronome still ticking, young Samuel Zwemer practically ran to the front to sign his name to a card, saying, "God helping me, I propose to be a foreign missionary." He didn't know it at the time, but years later he discovered that his mother had dedicated him to missionary service when he was an infant. His brother Peter also joined him in his commitment.

When asked where in the world he wanted to go, he declared in his youthful ardor that he wanted to go to the most difficult place on earth. After researching the matter, he determined that place would be with the Muslims in Saudi Arabia. They were the people most resistant to the gospel. As a friend of Zwemer's put it, "Of course that's where he was determined to go." He was just that kind of guy.

But no mission board would send him. "You'll be killed!" they told him. "We'll be sending you to die." So, being that kind of guy, Zwemer and his friend James Cantine started their own mission board, calling it the "Arabian Mission," and went out to raise support. Later, Zwemer would say,

"If God calls you to go to a place like Arabia and no mission board will send you, why, bore a hole through the board and go anyway."[22]

Zwemer spent his life in the cause of bringing Muslims to Christ and deserves more than a short chapter in this memoir. The distinguished mission historian, Kenneth Scott Latourette said of him, "No one through all the centuries of Christian missions to Muslims has deserved better than Samuel Zwemer the designation of Apostle to Islam."[23]

Indeed, many books have been written about him, and he wrote many books about missions. He was a bold entrepreneur, an incisive thinker, formidable in debate; a powerful speaker, prolific writer and, in the best sense of the word, as hardheaded and in-your-face a leader as you'd ever hope to meet. Or not want to meet.

For instance, in 1912 he stood in front of Al-Azhar University in Cairo, the preeminent theological school of Islam, and passed out Christian literature to students. He was reported to the British government for this transgression, which promptly kicked him out the country. He went to Cyprus for two weeks and then returned. British officials let the matter drop.

Besides his formidable tenacity, his friends all remarked about his infectious sense of humor. He could laugh, and make others laugh, even in Arabia, that most hostile-to-the-gospel place in the world. His friend Christy Wilson wrote, "If you read about what he did in Arabia, it was no wonder the people loved him."

His courage and commitment cost him dearly. His brother Peter died while they were on the mission field. Two daughters born to him and his wife Amy died of dysentery in July 1904. Their gravestone on the island of Bahrain reads, "Worthy is the Lamb to receive riches."

There is so much more to say about this towering figure, but I'll stop now and tell you why I'm talking about him. Before I came to Hope College in 1994, I had never heard of Samuel Zwemer. And after I arrived, it appeared that Hope College had never heard of him either. There was not a mention, not a plaque, not a word anywhere about him, outside the college archives. Maybe not there either, I don't know for sure. But publicly there was and is nothing anywhere on campus to visually draw attention to the man who is arguably one of the college's most eminent and illustrious graduates.[24]

Why is that? How did it happen?

The answer is in the things that happened after Duct-Tape Man sent a group of students on a mission trip to India. The story comes later in the chapter, "One Mountain, Many Paths?"

In the meantime God was quietly connecting the dots.

6

Connecting the Dots

The ancients gazed at the night sky and imagined the outlines of bears and dippers in the constellations—a big bear and a little bear, a big dipper and a little dipper.

My childhood was less imaginative. I liked to look at books with numbered dots. Connect them in numerical order and lo, a rooster, a bicycle, a smiley face.

Looking back at my time at Hope, I can see how David Bryant's charge and the dream I had on the north rim of the Grand Canyon were like those dots—on a much higher plane. There were other dots too, people especially. Seen together, all the dots make up a thumbnail sketch of what God was doing in the revival to bring Hope into his global purpose. They are related to each other not as cause and effect, but as the alignment of stars in a season, the Lord's season of revival and global impact.

There was Dolores Nasrallah.

As students began filling up the seats in chapel, Dolores began organizing them into small discipleship groups, training student leaders to lead them. The groups proliferated as new student disciples were making disciples. By the second year of the chapel ministry hundreds of students were growing in prayer and their grasp of the Scriptures. The net was cast wide, and many came in.

The obvious next step was to help these students connect their growing faith with God's global purpose. A chapel filled with worshipers every time its doors opened was thrilling and a lot of fun. That with the exponential growth of small groups to make disciples had us all buzzing with excitement. But as the Lord told me, that wasn't a big enough job.

Enter Lori Fair. She joined the staff to organize spring break and summer mission trips. The students' response to these trips was so enthusiastic early on that on one occasion students camped all night outside Lori's office to get in line for sign-ups. She had her hands happily full the next few years.

There was Barbara Yandell.

I met Barbara in 1989 when I became pastor of the Presbyterian Church in New Providence, New Jersey. When I arrived, she was a student at Gordon-Conwell Seminary, and had just finished an internship at the church. I believe she had been working with singles. More significantly, she had been praying for a spiritual awakening in the church. Later, she also helped me in Vision Ministries, a drive-time, Monday through Friday radio ministry I had in New York and Washington, DC. When she went off to finish her theological education, I thought that was the end of Barbara in my life. But there was more coming.

You need to know a little bit about what she is like. She is short and feisty. She's a Texan—attitude, accent, and all. She loves good food and hats. She's eccentric and opinionated in the best sense of the words—implacable, outspoken, courageous, and hilarious. She has a very big laugh. When she says, "Pay attention, y'all," you all best pay attention. She loves Christ and his kingdom, and she is a woman of prayer. And she just gets things done, behind the scenes, or in spite of the scenes, regardless of opposition. In short, she is not to be trifled with. And she is the last person you'd expect to see in the clerical robe of a Presbyterian clergyperson.

My wife, Lauretta, and I love her. She kept us sane and happy in the difficult times we had to face in the revival years. Sometimes she brought her sanity with a knock at the back door. We'd open the door, and there was Barbara standing on the doorstep with an apple pie in hand. Or cherry.

She deserves much more than a few paragraphs in this memoir. But keeping with the theme of God's oblique ways, the next thing I know Barbara is back in my life in Holland, Michigan. How she got there is beyond the scope of this story, but it is immensely interesting and encouraging to see how the Lord has led this woman and used her.

Judged simply by the numbers, her place in the "bigger" mission God was doing in the revival is impressive.

Beginning in 1996 and over the next twenty-one years she conducted twenty-one Perspectives on the World Christian Movement classes in Holland. And later in other places. Perspectives is an intensive series of lectures, readings and speakers on the theology, history, and practice of Christ's commission to make disciples of all peoples. It began with thirty-five Hope students meeting on campus. It expanded to include many other people and over the years, roughly nine hundred people attended Barbara's Perspectives classes.

Barbara also founded Hope for the Nations. Largely student led, it began with twenty-five students who came together weekly to study the Bible, pray for revival, and for men and women to be sent to evangelize the unreached peoples of the earth. Missions speakers spoke regularly. From year to year the composition of the group changed as students graduated from college. The majority of these students became missionaries, church leaders, pastors and house-church leaders. Many became involved in ministries of compassion in their communities. Hope for the Nations continues to this day.

Barbara's efforts were more than ancillary to what God was doing in the college revival. They were integral. In God's surreptitious mustard seed way, she was quietly and virtually everywhere, touching the lives of not just students, but people of all ages. Set next to the spectacular public face of the large chapel services, she can almost seem invisible. But without her, what we saw accomplished in a booming chapel attendance, would not have been a big enough job.

And significantly, she reintroduced the name Samuel Zwemer to the Hope College community. I had never heard of him before Barbara told me about him. And as I said in the previous chapter, it was as though Hope College, his alma mater, had never heard of him either. So I formed a prayer group for students discerning whether God might be calling them to global missions. I called it the Samuel Zwemer Fellowship.

There was also Barb Osburn.

I sure didn't see her coming either. Early on in our ministry, for a few months, my secretary Dani Hadley and I shared an office space with her in the wing of the administration building occupied by college advancement. We were waiting for the Keppel House on campus to be made ready for our own office. Barb was working in college advancement, that is, she was fundraising for Hope. I've since told her this, but when we first met she struck me as a well-dressed and articulate professional, who seemed very unhappy—which she was, as she later told me.

I didn't know it, but as soon as chapel services started, she started attending them regularly. She felt compelled to be there every time the doors of Dimnent opened. Fortunately, all college personnel were permitted to leave their jobs three times a week to attend the twenty-minute chapel services. She never missed one. She always sat in a section of chapel right behind where the basketball team sat. This went on for two years. As she put it, "God was doing deep surgery in my heart." Her life was thoroughly structured around her and her husband Paul's struggle to make ends meet financially. They had to have two incomes to live, they thought. There was no room for God in this densely packed schedule. Plus their marriage was struggling.

As she sat in chapel, she heard God's voice in her heart saying, "I love you so much. I have a much better life for you." She was beginning to surrender her life to Jesus. Her husband, Paul, came later. It's a great and inspiring story of healing and redemption.

It would have strained my credulity to the breaking point if you told me that the unhappy woman I first met in the college advancement office would one day join my staff as director of student missions! But that's what happened.

In 2000, Lori Fair decided it was time to move on to get more schooling. When Lori told me she was resigning from her student missions post, she and the staff and I talked about who might replace her. Barb Osburn's name came up, and the more we thought about her, the more sense she made. Between 2000 and 2010, Barb Osburn served as the director of student missions.

Barb was perfect for the job, if for no other reason, because her personal life quietly embodied God's greater purpose for the revival. Whenever I think of her I remember the prophetic words I heard as I left the New Providence church for Hope College. God told Isaiah that it wasn't a big enough job for him to merely "round up the strays of Israel" (Isaiah 49:6 The Message). Barb was one of the "strays" of Hope the Holy Spirit "rounded up." Now this former "stray" would be a part of his plan to round up more "strays" so that his salvation becomes global!

Early in her work she became friends with Barbara Yandell. She took Barbara's Perspectives course, and proceeded to take students or help students go on missions to places everywhere in the United States, as well as Mexico, Cuba, and Uganda. Not only was her marriage restored, it also became a mission in itself, as she and Paul adopted internationally—four children from Ethiopia, and three from Burma became part of the Osburn clan. And, oh yes, they also managed to raise three strapping biological sons.

Paul became a beloved spiritual father to many. We were shocked and devastated when he suddenly died from a rare and aggressive form of leukemia, December 16, 2022. The memory of his godly strength and fatherly compassion animates a continued commitment of the Osburn family to fulfill Christ's commission to make disciples of all peoples. Barb remains a precious friend.

The First One to Wake Up in a Spiritual Awakening

It was a season of joyful expectancy. The trajectory of the spiritual awakening was steep and surging. Interest in prayer, missions, evangelism, service, Bible study, and worship grew, as many experienced the simple joys of a community enjoying a heightened sense of the enlivening presence of God.

But something else was growing and surging too, something contra revival from the beginning, something parallel and simultaneously opposed to what God was doing. I believe it was Dwight L. Moody who said, "The first one to wake up in a spiritual awakening is the devil." Provocative as it is, I'll use that phrase to introduce the next section of this memoir. But with this caveat: I do not believe—I repeat—I do not believe that those opposed to what was happening spiritually were the devil or necessarily of the devil. Whether any of the opposition were actually of the devil only God knows. I don't, and I won't speculate who it might be. But I will insist that there was a war going on from the beginning, a spiritual war. As Scripture says, "Our struggle is not against flesh and blood but . . . . against the powers of this dark world and against the spiritual forces of evil in the heavenly realms" (Ephesians 6:12). As John White put it, spiritual warfare is not a metaphor, it is literally the reality of the world we live in:

> War is not something that illustrates aspects of Christian living. Christian living *is* war. Indeed, I would go further. Earthly warfare is not the real warfare. It is but a faint, ugly reflection of the real thing. It is into the *real* war that the Christian is to plunge. Wars on earth are but tremors felt from an earthquake light-years away. The Christian's war takes place at the epicenter of the earthquake. It is infinitely more deadly, while the issues that hang on it make earth's most momentous questions no more than village gossip.[25]

Because the warfare is spiritual, the weapons are too; things like prayer, the Word of God, faith, hope, truth, and love.

> For though we live in the world, we do not wage war as the world does. The weapons we fight with are not the weapons of the world. On the contrary, they have divine power to demolish strongholds. We demolish arguments and every pretension that sets itself up against the knowledge of God, and we take captive every thought to make it obedient to Christ.[26]

When I arrived at Hope, I had clearly entered a spiritual war zone. I sensed it from the beginning, most pointedly in the fallout from a faculty luncheon, September 27, 1994.

7

"We Will Stonewall You"

Or, Welcome to the Big Tent

It was the best of times, it was the worst of times.
—Charles Dickens, *A Tale of Two Cities*

All who would be faithful followers of Jesus in our advanced modern world . . . must become impossible people—Christians with hearts that can melt with compassion, but with faces like flint and backbones of steel who are unmanipulable, unbribable, undeterrable and unclubbable,[27] without ever losing the gentleness, the mercy, the grace and the compassion of our Lord.

—Os Guinness

M y family and I received a warm and enthusiastic welcome to Hope College, when we first arrived just before Christmas 1993. Right away we enjoyed Hope's spectacular Christmas Vespers celebration—one of the college's richest and most beloved traditions.

I was dazzled.

Welcome to the Big Tent

Among the many people I met was a prominent leader in both the academic community of Holland and the Reformed Church of America. A learned and hospitable man, he had lots of friends in the faculties of Hope College and Western Seminary, both of which he had served in for years and was still serving with distinction. He had a lot of friends and he wanted me to know this community was a "big tent"—that there would be lots of room for someone like me with my particular theological convictions, and I shouldn't feel like a stranger.

I was encouraged.

So I thought, this would be a good time to tell him a bit about my theological convictions. I asked him, how would I fit in at Hope—I searched for the right words—as an "evangelical Christian" (still the first word that comes to mind)? And I quickly added, "but definitely not a fundamental-ist," though I told him that, for a significant time in my younger years, "fun-damentalist" would have been a badge I wore with pride. Then I described the impact of two books I read as a first-year college student, that changed my life. They were, *The Case for Orthodox Theology*, by Edward John Carnell, and *Mere Christianity* by C. S. Lewis. I told him how the narrowness and ri-gidity of my "fundamentalist" beliefs had matured into orthodoxy, not as in Eastern Orthodoxy, but as in the historic faith of the church—what Chris-tians have believed in all times and all places, conservative and ancient, but ever new—what Lewis called Mere Christianity. And didn't Hope College declare itself as operating in the context of the historic Christian faith? I told him I delighted in the "historic faith" part, though I wondered about what the "context" part meant.

Encouraged in my zeal I waxed eloquent as he listened and smiled and nodded his head approvingly. "Yes, yes," he said. "Be fully who you are! Be an evangelical. Don't hold back. Hope College is a Big Tent, there's room for you here."

And I believed him.

Early in the first semester of that first year at Hope, Jack Nyenhuis, the college provost, said to me, "Why don't you share your vision for the chapel ministry at the faculty luncheon this week? I'll introduce you at the end of lunch. Make it short, just ten minutes."

The date was September 27, 1994, the end of the first month of chapel services.

I was excited about the opportunity. Everything was fresh and new. This would be my first exposure to the Hope faculty as a group.

We Are Far Too Easily Pleased

Summarizing your vision is always a good exercise for a leader, I thought. What were the irreducible minimums of the things I prayed God would do in my work as Hope College's first dean of the chapel? Make it all fit on a 3X5 card. I would speak simply from my heart about what I believed was my mission. I was confident the faculty would be excited too. I really was. Who wouldn't be excited about what I was praying for God to do? They could pray with me.

I truly believed they might.

I had two points. The first had to do with the spiritual life of the com-

We Will Stonewall You

munity. I told them I was praying for a spiritual awakening on campus like the one the apostle Paul prayed for the Ephesians, that we would have power, "to grasp how wide and long and high and deep is the love of Christ, and to know this love that surpasses knowledge" (Ephesians 3:18–19).

I told the faculty that I envisioned a college community with a pervasive sense of the goodness and presence of God. I urged them to imagine what it would be like to be all that God made us to be, that there is so much more to life in the Spirit than we have yet even to imagine, that God's chief complaint with his people is not that we want too much, but that we are satisfied with too little. As I was to do often with students in the next seven years, I quoted what for me were a few lines from a life-changing essay by C. S. Lewis's essay, *The Weight of Glory*:

> If we consider the unblushing promises of reward and the staggering nature of the rewards promised in the Gospels, it would seem that Our Lord finds our desires not too strong, but too weak. We are half-hearted creatures, fooling about with drink and sex and ambition when infinite joy is offered us, like an ignorant child who wants to go on making mud pies in a slum because he cannot imagine what is meant by the offer of a holiday at the sea. We are far too easily pleased.[28]

I admitted that yes, that's a lot to ask God for. But why not ask for what he has assured us he wants to give? What greater blessing could fall on a largely residential community like Hope College?

I really believed they would be excited at the prospect of this. I truly did.

I Ended Provocatively

My second point had to do with the academic side of the Hope community. I said I was praying that we would experience a renewal—a deepening sense of Christian vocation in the life of the mind. The Dutch thinker Abraham Kuyper would be a great place to start. He said, "There is not a square inch in the whole domain of our human existence over which Christ, who is Sovereign over all, does not cry, Mine!" Surely a faculty at a college connected with the Reformed tradition had heard of him. I said, "I can't tell you chemistry professors what it means for people in the discipline of chemistry to say, 'Christ is Lord,' but I can invite you into the adventure of discovering what it means." And so for all the disciplines—art, literature, history, philosophy, biology or anything else Hope teaches and trains students for—we could pray that the knowledge of God would fill the campus like the waters cover the sea. I prayed that students and faculty would discover how the glory of God can "flame out like shining from shook foil"[29] in even a classroom or a laboratory.

I ended provocatively. I said that if we believe all creation belongs to Christ, a Christian can never compartmentalize. For us there can therefore be no sacred/secular division because for a believer, all of life, including every academic pursuit is ultimately a religious matter. In that sense—and here comes the whammy—Hope College should not see itself as an academic institution with a religious dimension, but as the reverse: a religious institution with an academic dimension. After all, it billed itself as a Christian college, didn't it? How could it be otherwise, if we believe, as the Scripture says, "The earth is the Lord's and everything in it" (1 Corinthians 10:26)? I had no idea how provocative, actually how inflammatory, that phrase was—"a religious institution with an academic dimension."

I Was Honestly Shocked

It was very quiet in the room when I finished. When I asked if there were any questions, it seemed to get quieter. No one responded to my invitation. I honestly feared they were bored by my vision. Maybe they were so familiar with it, maybe it was so basic, so much a given, that they couldn't think of anything to ask or say.

Later I asked Nyenhuis if my remarks were too pedestrian to elicit any excitement. He shook his head and said, "No, not at all. They were silent because they couldn't believe you would say something like that."

I was honestly shocked by what he said. I eventually learned there had been a long-standing debate within the community about the college's faculty hiring policy; heated debates over whether the faculty should include non-Christians. There were more than a few nonbelievers on the faculty, and there were also more than a few self-identified believers, usually what one would term "liberals," who believed it didn't matter what a professor believed about the faith, as long as they were competent in their discipline. I would come to call them the revisionists. Over time, I preferred the nonbelievers to the revisionists. The nonbelievers were easier to get along with.

I knew nothing of this when I spoke; I was naively and blissfully ignorant of the debate. I'm glad I was—not that knowing this would have changed what I said, but not knowing made it easier to be authentically and innocently carefree and enthusiastic when I gave my little talk. I had fun sharing my vision with the faculty. I felt playful in an earnest sort of way.

One of the faculty called me immediately afterward for an appointment. The only thing I knew about him, other than his discipline in the social sciences, was that he seemed to be on the inside of a group of influential faculty at Hope. Or at least he thought himself to be. He had reached out to me soon after I arrived on campus, and seemed anxious to fill me in on some inside information about the college. He certainly spoke to me as one who believed he carried that kind of authority. He even invited my wife and me to dinner and an awkward evening with another faculty member.

He entered my office, sat down and went abruptly to the point of our meeting. He let me know that what I envisioned for Hope College was not the "Hope way." He used that term several times. Didn't I know that a significant number of the faculty were not Christians? What would they think of a chapel dean who promoted a pervasive sense of the presence of Christ? For that matter, he said I needed to know that even those faculty who self-identified as Christian weren't warm to the idea of my kind of religion either. He obviously thought himself to be one of that kind. He took particular umbrage at the implication that I thought Hope College needed a spiritual awakening. The phrase he repeated over and over was, "religious life here is not moribund." This professor liked the word "moribund" a lot. And it was clear that by "religious life" he meant religion in general, not the Christian faith in particular. As he saw it, the existing chapel ministry was just fine.

I don't recall him asking me any questions. He just talked and talked, and concluded: "You will be here for just a while and eventually leave. But we will still be here after you leave. And we will stonewall you."

A Neighborhood Bully

I assumed the "we" he referred to were close friends who knew and embraced the "Hope way," whatever that was. That last phrase, "We will stonewall you," reverberated in my mind for the next seven years as I served at Hope College. They still do. He could not have chosen words more certain to make me stiffen my back and think, "Well, bring it on."

He brought back a memory from my childhood of a neighborhood bully on a bicycle yelling at me to get out of the way.

I couldn't have been much more than five years old, and he was a really big kid, maybe seven or eight, and he could ride a *two-wheel* bicycle. None of my friends or I could do this, so we held him in awe, and he knew it. Whenever my buddies and I would play a game on the sidewalk, he'd get on his bicycle and ride as fast as he could, right down the middle of the sidewalk in our direction, screaming for us to get out of the way. He was terrifying on that big two-wheeler, and we scrambled frantically to get out of his way.

But with each humiliation my resentment grew. I didn't know what the word injustice meant, but I was learning what it felt like. It wasn't right that he had his fun bullying us. So one day I decided not to move when he bore down on us at top speed. I stood up, planted my feet and faced him, not so tall but righteous and proud.

And he ran over me.

Two things stood out about the collision. One was how surprised I was at how much it hurt to get run over. The other was that he got hurt too, even more than me. The impact also sent him crashing to the pavement. I remember lying on the sidewalk, my breath knocked out of me, gasping for air, unable even to cry. That was bad; it was the most pain I had ever experienced in my young life. But I also heard him *wailing* in pain and rage! And when I looked, I saw him lying a few feet away, his knees skinned up and his forehead bleeding. I thought, this is good! And it got even better when I saw his mother, who had witnessed the whole incident, run over and scold him for what he did.

I limped home in triumph, with the germ of an idea in my mind that I've reflected on and tried to live by ever since. What I did was hard to do, so hard that I'd think twice before I did it again. But what I had been suffering at the hands of that little terrorist was hard too, harder actually. The choice had not been whether to do a hard thing, but which hard thing; the good hard or the bad hard. That experience imprinted itself on my consciousness, and has shaped my approach to bullies and hostile challenges ever since. If something is going to be hard, I want it to be a good hard.

A Long Line of Pugilists

It reinforced what my father's courage and steadfastness had been teaching me all along. My dad was a fighter. A child of the Great Depression in the 1930s, he had grown up in poverty and fought his way through adversity to work and provide for his family. He had even been a boxer for a while, and had a misshapen nose to prove it. He would comment about himself, sometimes ruefully, "You may be able to lead me over a cliff, but you can never push me over." He admitted he could be deceived, but never coerced. I grew up thinking it was manly to stand up and fight for what I believed was right. It even felt good, in an uncomfortable sort of way. The one sport I excelled in was football, as an undersized interior lineman.

At Hope, in the years that followed I had abundant opportunities to be steadfast and immovable. John Jacobson, the president who hired me, recalls me saying, "I come from a long line of pugilists."[30] Again, something I don't remember saying, but true. Some used that trait as an ad hominem argument against my convictions and the stands I took; that I did what I did more out of congenital combativeness and cussedness, than thoughtful conviction—just another "fighting fundamentalist." Truthfully, I wasn't always sure myself which it was. Was I courageous or just pigheaded and stubborn? Whatever the truth is, that character trait helped me stand my ground when my convictions were tested. This is not to say that I was always a righteous or courageous fighter. But I had come to believe that God is never on the side of the coward.

I had already begun to feel an outsider at Hope. The way he lectured me increased the alien experience. I thought, if he and his posse were the "inside," I didn't want to be on the inside. The last thing I wanted to do was hang out with this crowd. It was a visceral feeling.

If I had to, I could be "impossible," a "stonewall" too, like Jeremiah, "a fortified city, an iron pillar and a bronze wall to stand against the whole land" (Jeremiah 1:18).

But there was more. What he said gave credence to something a friend of mine named Jack Serra said to me shortly after I arrived at Hope. He belonged to what I jokingly called "the people of the charismatic persuasion." He embraced the label and we laughed about it. Jack actually believed God speaks to people. So after praying for me and with me about my assignment at Hope, for a few days, he gently and tentatively offered me what he sensed the Holy Spirit had said to him about my work at the college. It was, "Tell Ben he needs to remain an outsider there. If he becomes an insider he will compromise his mission and lose his effectiveness."

I didn't want to hear that. I certainly didn't answer God's call to come to Hope with the idea that I needed to be something of an outsider. But I have learned over the years not to dismiss out of hand words like these, but to wait and see.

I didn't have to wait long to see more. Soon after my meeting with Mr. Stonewall, I saw two more things I would have to stand against, both on the same night, during the first semester of our work.

8

A Prayer Meeting on Porn Night
Fall, 1994

A huge door of opportunity for good work has opened up here.
(There is also mushrooming opposition.)
—1 Corinthians 16:9 (The Message)

Everything, Everywhere, All at Once
—the title of the 2023 Oscar-winning motion picture

S oon after the "stonewall" meeting, three or four male students asked if
I would meet with them for prayer in their dorm room.

What I saw as I approached their room was the last thing I expected
to see.

And I heard it before I saw it. Raucous hoots and shouts and applause
were erupting out of a crowd massed around an open door in a dorm room
just two doors down from the students I came to pray with. The young men
were craning their necks and jumping up to see what was going on inside. I
thought it might be some sporting event, and I almost asked someone what
the score was. As I passed, I, too, craned my neck to see what was happening
inside. What I saw flickering on a big television screen was a hard-core porn
movie. I quickly turned away, hoping no one might think I was trying to get
a peek too.

The students I went to pray with told me that porn movies were a regular occurrence on a night the other students in the dorm called "porn night."
That was the reason they asked me to come and pray with them. They said it
always happened in full view of anyone who might be walking by. The door
was always open on "porn night." No one worried that anyone in charge of
things would be alarmed. I had already remarked to myself that if anyone
in the crowd saw the new dean of the chapel passing through, they didn't
appear to be embarrassed or even interested in my presence. They seemed
used to adults around the edges of their goings on, unconcerned about their
behavior.

So I prayed that night with a little group of nervous and dispirited Christian students in their dorm room. Their door was closed, but the sounds of "porn night," blaring a few feet away, provided a kind of infernal, mocking soundtrack to our prayers for a spiritual awakening at Hope College. As we prayed, and tried to block out the enormous distraction of the spectacle next door, I tried to read their faith thermometer. How were they doing? I had to admit to myself that if prayer had ever seemed weak and ineffectual to me, it did then. It felt like spitting into the wind.

An hour before, I had actually been unwittingly prepared for "porn night" by a conversation I had with one of the dorm's resident assistants. I asked him for an informal tour of the dorm, and as he showed me around I noticed a note taped over a drinking fountain. In large letters, it read, "Don't spit in the fountain, it's f***ing disgusting."

I asked him what he thought of the note.

With a look I couldn't distinguish from baffled or amused, he asked, "What do you mean?"

I said, "I'm not your boss and I can't tell you what to do, but do you think a note like that should be hanging in the residence hall of a Christian college?"

He paused for a moment and studied my face to see, I suppose, if my question was serious. Then he shrugged quizzically and motioned for me to follow him as he continued to show me around.

So the evening began with the "F" word episode. It continued with "porn night" two doors down from a prayer meeting. And it ended on a similar note after the prayer meeting.

One more revelation awaited. As I walked out of the dorm into the night, I noticed that one of the student development staff was conducting a seminar in the dorm lounge. A big hand-drawn sign advertised it as something like, "Gays and Lesbians: Why They Can't Be Like the Rest of Us." Since the meeting was just ending, I waited for the last student to leave, and asked the man who was leading the seminar what his message was.

I could tell he was nervous about the question, and who was asking it. He hesitated, and explained that he was urging students to see people with those particular sexual attractions and practices as okay, just the way they are; not deviant, not bad, just different. And that they should not be judged, but affirmed and supported in the ways they express their sexual identity.

I asked him to clarify what he meant by, "not bad, just different." Was he promoting what we often called then a "pro-gay" position? He said he was.

Exactly as I had with the resident assistant and the "F" word note, I began my response with, "I'm not your boss, and I can't tell you what to do." I continued with, "I'm sure there a lot of families who sent their sons and daughters to Hope College who have no idea that a seminar like yours would be offered with the college's sanction. I think they would be very upset if they knew that a member of the student development staff was promoting what you promoted tonight."

Let me explain something about what it has been like trying to write in 2023 about that evening in 1994.

Amid all the short naps, walks around the block, aimless wanderings around the house and rummagings through the refrigerator and pantry for snacks and other forms of procrastination, it took hours to write just a paragraph about it. How do I describe the encounter that evening with what became the most explosive issue in my time at Hope? How can I speak into the enormous issue it has become in our culture today, yet not appear to be the bigot or homophobe I was accused of being in the '90s?

It can't be done. So here goes, anyway.

Quite simply, I believe that the historic teaching of the church, throughout its twenty centuries has spoken with virtually one voice about the things Scripture condemns as sin. These include homosexual behavior. It is sin, not worse than all the others, but like all the others, just plain old sin—things like lust, adultery, malice, greed, hatred, covetousness, murder, disobedience to parents, deceit, and envy.[31] We are all fallen and broken people, living in a broken and fallen world. We have all sinned and all fall short of the glory of God. The Bible speaks the bad news about us all, and the good news of God for us all in the same breath. The wages of sin is death, but the gift of God is eternal life through Jesus Christ.[32]

You may accuse me of bigotry, but your argument is not with me, but with Scripture. Worse, to argue that Scripture doesn't actually teach what it clearly teaches (as some have argued) is to argue not against a particular truth but truth itself and to call black, white. It's devilish. The church father Irenaeus saw this clearly.

> Error, indeed, is never set forth in its naked deformity lest, being thus exposed it should at once be detected. But it is craftily decked out in an attractive dress so as, by its outward form to make it appear to the inexperienced more true than truth itself.[33]

Significantly, my main objection to what was going on in the dorm on porn night, and in that seminar was the breach of faith with many families that send their children to Hope. It was a covert undermining of their children's faith.

I soon received another call requesting an appointment—not from this man's supervisor, the dean of students, but from a psychology professor. I don't remember the specific language she used when we met, but her anger was palpable, not so much in her words, but in her face and the terse way she questioned me about my theology. She let me know that a person with my beliefs about human sexuality was not what "they" were looking for in a dean of the chapel. Unlike the sociology professor who threatened that he and his colleagues would "stonewall" me, she made no threats. But it was clear that she was one of them, whoever they were. Over the next few years I encountered her and the work of the "stonewall" gang over and over again. Their resistance was usually covert in the beginning, often resorting to malicious gossip and backbiting. But toward the end of my time at Hope it became nakedly aggressive.

If the meeting with the professor was hostile, the evasive response of the student development office, which sponsored the seminar, was hypocritical. The dean protested that he had no knowledge of a regular event called "porn night." He dismissed it as just one of those things some students may do from time to time—as though the random nature of this kind of thing was nothing to be grieved over. As for the "seminar" on homosexuality, he said his office's approach to this issue was to help students think independently about this matter, and be guided by whatever their personal beliefs were—not the teaching of Scripture, but just what they felt—as though the seminar his office sponsored wasn't the advocacy event it actually was.

This initial disparity in belief and perspective between my office and the student development office more than set the tone of the relationship between my office and that office for the seven years I spent at Hope.

We Had Infiltrated

When I got home that night, I marveled that so much darkness would come to light on a night that a beleaguered little prayer group met to pray for the college. We felt surrounded by all that raunchy noise! We could hardly hear each other speak. We felt impotent and negligible. But then it occurred to me that, unaware, we had been calling on the name of the Lord from the belly of the beast! We weren't surrounded, we had infiltrated. The prayer meeting was a spiritual stealth mission! Of course vile things were exposed! Prayer sends searing light into the darkness and the darkness cannot stand it. Though we may not see it, prayer is as disruptive of the powers of darkness as what happened when Jesus sent a legion of demons out of a demonized man into a herd of pigs, and the crazed beasts stampeded into a lake and drowned.[34] As George Herbert put it, prayer is "reversed thunder."[35] A prayer meeting may be quiet and sedate, but in the unseen world there is thunder, lightning and earthquakes.[36]

The redoubtable missionary Mary Slessor—a spunky little woman who worked mostly alone, rescuing orphans in Africa in the nineteenth century—knew this. In letters sent home to friends and family, she testified that "prayer is the greatest power God has put into our hands for service. Praying is harder work than doing . . . but the dynamic lies that way to advance the kingdom."[37]

So—between the "stonewall" threat, and the porn night miasma—the main trajectories of conflict and redemption in the chapel ministry for the years ahead were now revealed, all within a few weeks of my first semester at Hope. Eventually severe conflict would erupt publicly around matters of human sexuality, theological orthodoxy and the meaning of Christian higher education. But for now the conflict was just beginning to simmer, uncomfortably. In the future it would explode with rage and rancor. I could see it coming. In a sense, that is how it should be; because the issues that divided us were about truth and falsehood, life and death. Forever. Literally.

You Can Postpone the Inevitable, But You Cannot Avoid It

Following Jesus Christ will surely bring us face-to-face with conflict. As C. S. Lewis remarked, "We may note in passing that He was never regarded as a great moral teacher. He did not produce that effect on any of the people who actually met Him. He produced mainly three effects—Hatred—Terror—Adoration. There was no trace of people expressing mild approval."[38] Nor was there any trace of "mild disapproval" either, not only for Jesus, but also for his followers. There would be tribulation. It goes with the territory. The Lord warned that, "If they beat on me, they will certainly beat on you" (John 15:20 The Message).

9

A Place to Stand

Life can only be understood backward; but it must be lived forward.
—Soren Kierkegaard

Give me but one firm spot on which to stand, and I will move the earth.
—Archimedes

"Not by might nor by power, but by my Spirit," says the LORD Almighty.
—Zechariah 4:6

If you build it, he will come.
—Field of Dreams

Tremors of great future conflict began almost immediately after I started my work at Hope College. Being told by a professor, "We will stonewall you," was a portent of things to come. So was praying for a spiritual awakening with the soundtrack of a porn movie in the background, and a seminar promoting the legitimacy of the LGBT[39] lifestyle going on downstairs.

I wasn't surprised.

Louis Evans Jr., my first boss, mentor, and dear friend gave me great advice about navigating the hard parts of ministry. Just before this remarkable man retired as a pastor, I asked him teasingly over dinner what wisdom he had to impart about my future service to Christ, before he "went out to pasture." We could rib each other that way. He hardly looked up from his plate before he took his next bite and answered, "Don't take it personally."

"Don't take what personally?" I asked.

He replied, "Don't take it personally when ministry is hard, when you get hammered with criticism and discouragement. It goes with the territory. You're at war."

The Narrow Way

What he said made sense. When a soldier is shot at by the enemy, he doesn't stick his head out over the foxhole and shout back, "Was it something I said?" It doesn't hurt his feelings, he expects it; it's the kind of thing that happens in wars.

When I heard Louis's words I blushed to think of how often I had reacted to hardship as though the struggle was about me—my strengths and weaknesses, my character and wisdom, *my feelings*. Functionally, I defined hardship as people and circumstances making me feel bad. His advice reminded me that I needed to get over myself, and my preoccupation with how I was experiencing things. I am a soldier in a spiritual war. I shouldn't be hurt and disappointed when the work is difficult; I should expect the hardness, even embrace it, because it's part of the narrow way Jesus said leads to life.[40] The early Puritans understood this. They knew, as James Packer wrote, that

> ease and luxury, such as our affluence brings us today, do not make for maturity; hardship and struggles do, and . . . . they accepted conflict as their calling, seeing themselves as their Lord's soldier pilgrims, . . . not expecting to be able to advance a single step without opposition of one sort or another.[41]

I've kept that quote on my desk for years. Louis Evans Jr., James Packer, and the Puritans were only echoing the words of Scripture which says that all Christian believers are, in fact, embroiled in a cosmic spiritual conflict. Holy Scripture says so:

> Finally, be strong in the Lord and in his mighty power. Put on the full armor of God so that you can take your stand against the devil's schemes. For our struggle is not against flesh and blood, but against the rulers, against the authorities, against the powers of this dark world, and against the spiritual forces of evil in the heavenly realms. (Ephesians 6:10–12)

We Have Met the Enemy and He Is Us

For most of my ministry I thought that if I did things right, there would be no conflict. I assumed that if things became difficult it must be because

I was doing something wrong. But then I learned that it might mean the opposite; it might mean that I was doing something right and that I was advancing into enemy territory.

But a caveat is in order here. This isn't to say that I didn't have to reckon with my own incompetence and depravity in this spiritual warfare. For even when it is my bad judgment or character that is at fault, it just means that my heart is part of the problem, a part of the enemy territory to be conquered. The Heidelberg Catechism explains that our Lord's command to pray to be delivered from sin and evil means more than to be saved from the devil's wiles and the world's darkness. It also means to pray to be saved from our own sinfulness, what the Scripture calls our "flesh."

> By ourselves we are too weak to hold our own even for a moment. And our sworn enemies—the devil, the world, and our own flesh— never stop attacking us. And so, Lord uphold us and make us strong with the strength of your Holy Spirit so that we may not go down to defeat in this spiritual struggle but may firmly resist our enemies until we finally win the complete victory.

Walt Kelley's famous quip put it this way: "We have met the enemy and he is us." My darkened heart can be one of the big three sworn enemies of God's kingdom—standing side by side with the devil and the world. To live for Christ is to fight our enemies, even when the enemy is ourselves.

So, even though I had come to expect some conflict in Christian ministry, I was surprised at how quickly conflict came at Hope and how vociferous it was. I didn't know who or how many were in the "stonewall" group, but I sensed their numbers might be large or very influential. I never found out how many, but I soon found out how influential they were.

Irreconcilable Differences—Three Preeminent Truths

We had much to argue about.

What were the issues? In one way or another they all emanated from irreconcilable theological differences regarding three preeminent truths: what is the very heart and essence of the historic Christian faith, what is the authority of Scripture and what it means to be a human being, to bear the image of God, the *imago Dei*, especially in the realm of sexuality.

Other people who lived through those days might substitute or add to these three. Some insisted that the problem stemmed mainly from the stubborn and irascible character of the dean of the chapel (me). There were also complaints from some circles about what they considered to be the shallow contemporary Christian music we sang in chapel—what some called "Christian-Lite." Swirled throughout were differing views about the place of Christian faith in academe and fiercely held faculty opinions about the limits (if any) of academic freedom. These all played a role in the disputes, but I will insist, as I did then, that the ultimate, fundamental bone of contention was what are the fundamentals of the Christian faith—regarding the faith, the Bible, and the *imago Dei* as expressed in human sexuality.

Part of me wanted to get on with the arguing, the sooner the better. Threats like, "we will stonewall you" will, over time, breed malice and muttering among all involved. Like a credit card bill—it's pay now or pay later, with compounded interest. And did we ever pay later, when the conflict broke out publicly.

But for the time being I groaned. The "time being" was my first year as chapel dean. The last thing I wanted to deal with was open conflict. Though open conflict was inevitable, and I think necessary, my prayer was that it be postponed until the chapel ministry was more established.

A Place to Stand and Spread Our Sails

To get there, my staff and I needed to find a place to stand: metaphorically what Archimedes was describing when he said, "Give me but one firm spot on which to stand, and I will move the earth." The Greek philosopher/scientist was thinking of how a well-placed fulcrum and lever are tools that can be used to move loads many times their size and weight.

My staff and I needed to establish something like that, a way of life that would work like a fulcrum, to move the ministry forward at Hope. Our life together would be the lever and fulcrum, the Spirit of God would be the hand that presses and moves the work. As always, people, not programs are God's method. There is no technique or "rule" that in itself has power to move God's Kingdom forward. From first to last, it is the power of the Holy Spirit working through his people, that moves the world—or a campus.

The metaphor isn't perfect. Another way to picture how God works through people is this: Jesus said the Holy Spirit cannot be harnessed and controlled. He is like the wind. He blows when and where he wills. Though we cannot control the wind, we can spread our sails to be moved when the wind does blow. We can position ourselves to receive the Spirit's power. For the Spirit is eager to blow his life-giving power into his church, and through his church into the world. This was what I had been learning to do in the churches I pastored over the years before I came to Hope. *I was finding a place to stand firm in readiness, not to move the Spirit, but for the Spirit to move us.*

The Three P's

What had I been learning? As I got older, it got simpler—because I got simpler.

We would remember to do just three things: Preach, Pray, and Pastor in the power of the Holy Spirit.

Although I didn't call them this at the time, I would come to call them the three *P*'s. These three not only embodied the main things I wanted to see happen with students, but it also set the agenda for what had to happen with my staff and me. Jesus said as much when he prayed that his disciples be one as he and his Father are one. He declared this unity would actually convince the world that his Father had sent him and loved the church as he loved his Son.[42] What we sought for the students, we sought to be together.

So we practiced these three things.

We Preached in the power of the Holy Spirit. We held the Scriptures, the Word of God, preeminent in chapel, and in all our dealings with each other and the college community. We preached the Word to the students, and we preached the Word to each other, as the Spirit empowered us. The ways we preached were especially, but not only, from the pulpit, but also in our singing.

We Prayed in the power of the Holy Spirit. We constantly and relentlessly called on the name of the Lord, to send the fullness of his Spirit to Hope and to our little band of chaplains. Writer Anne Lamott once said her prayer life came down to two prayers: In the morning she prayed, "Help me, help me, help me"; in the evening it was, "Thank you, thank you, thank you." That was us. Our days began and ended with those two prayers. The Scriptures say, "Unless the Lord builds the house, the work of the builders is wasted" (Psalm 127:1 NLT). We believed that. So we prayed daily help us, help us!" And accordingly we found ourselves a over and over again, with thanksgiving and awe, "Thank you, thank you!"

I read somewhere that Lamott eventually added a third prayer to her life liturgy of "Help me!" and "Thank you!" It was "Wow!" That was us too.

We Pastored in the power of the Holy Spirit. The third *P* needs a little explaining, because I have come to think and speak of it in a way that probably seems puzzling and a little quirky. To pastor Hope students, we needed to pastor each other. That meant we needed to pray with and for each other. Much of that meant to "waste time" with students and with each other. There's a story behind the phrase, "waste time."

It's an important story.

The first church I pastored was a church start-up in Irvine, California. It began in 1975 with a nucleus of mainly young families, and a handful of students at the University of California at Irvine. Over the next fourteen years we grew steadily into a congregation of six or seven hundred. I can gauge our growth by photos of the beautiful (to us) and rambunctious children who were born and grew up in our midst. Actually it was also the photos of my wife and me as we grew and matured in service to Christ. Those years together were sweet—not without the same tensions common to any community made up of sinners being saved and sanctified by the Holy Spirit—but tender and vibrant and alive in faith, hope, and love.

The Lord called me away to serve a church in New Providence, New Jersey, in 1989. After I was there two years, the Irvine Church invited me to come back and preach for a weekend. It was to be a happy reunion with old friends and family. I couldn't wait to see them all again.

But one thing disturbed me when I came back to Irvine. I looked around at what was going on in the church, and I couldn't find one program I had started in the church. I had been gone only two years, and it seemed as though everything I had worked so hard to build was gone. At first my feelings were hurt and I was a little mad. The Lord let me stew in my resentment and disappointment for a few hours. Then his Spirit pointed out the people who had been leading the church and loving its people the past two years. Almost all of them were folks I had "wasted time" with. That is, I had spent a lot of time with them not getting anything done, and it often seemed at the time that I was wasting time. All I was doing was loving them and walking with them in the day-to-day events of life. "All were doing was loving them," the Holy Spirit said. The tone wasn't sarcastic, but it could have been. I was reminded that ministry is usually inefficient. Like raising children. It's loving presence, the sacrament of the ordinary and the mundane.

I told the Lord, "I don't know how many years I have left, but I want to spend the rest of my time serving you by 'wasting time' with people." It was 1992, and I write this in 2023, thirty-one years later. Thank you, Jesus! When I got to Hope, I wanted to "waste time" with students, my staff, and whoever God brought to me. And we did it together.

We devoted ourselves to these happy practices as we waited expectantly for the wind of the Spirit to blow at Hope. None of these practices or postures, in and of themselves, had the power to change Hope College. Call them means of grace or habits of grace or whatever—the main thing is the Holy Spirit works in and through these practices the way wind blows into a sail. From beginning to end, it was "not by might, not by power, but by my Spirit, says the LORD Almighty"(Zechariah 4:6).

Looking back on those days, I remember the 1989 movie classic, "Field of Dreams," which came out five years before we began our work. It was the story of Ray Kinsella, a novice Iowa farmer who heard a voice urging him to build a baseball field in his cornfield. The voice said, "If you build it, he will come." Just who the "he" was who would come, and the "they" who would come with him, is a lovely and touching fantasy about the healing of a man's soul. Finding a place to stand in the ministry at Hope was a little like that, but no fantasy. The One who came in power was the One who told us to spread our sails.

I believed God had uniquely called me to Hope College to lead a staff to do a work of the Holy Spirit in the specific ways my staff and I stood and spread our sails together. I will talk about them in chapters to come.

The Three Markers

But I need to go back to the story of what happened to me in the months before I got to Hope.

Before I even met the people I would preach, pray, and pastor with, there were three distinct messages and experiences God gave me in the months before I arrived at the college. Remarkably each was a sign of what was to come at Hope and who I needed to be—all within less than nine months before I stepped onto the campus. Although I didn't see any of them that way when they came to me, I look back on them as divine foreshadowings, instances of Danish philosopher Soren Kierkegaard's aphorism, "Life can only be understood backward; but it must be lived forward." I surely needed to look back and remember them in the seven years I served as dean of the chapel. Henry Blackaby calls them "markers."

I've already written about two markers: One: a certain sense that had definitely called me to serve him at Hope ("Remember When You Thought You Wanted to Work with College Students?"). Two: a charge to see the work as global in scope ("That's Not a Big Enough Job"). Both would require unbending toughness and determination to fulfill.

The third marker was an experience of being held in love by the Holy Spirit to sustain me.

10

Something Like a Language

(Held in Love, part 1)

We are enfolded in the Father, and we are enfolded in the Son, and we are enfolded in the Holy Spirit. And the Father is enfolded in us, and the Son is enfolded in us, and the Holy Spirit is enfolded in us: almightiness, all wisdom, all goodness: one God, one Lord.

—Julian of Norwich

T his third marker happened to me in November 1993, just before I left the Presbyterian Church I was pastoring in New Jersey to go to Hope College. I discovered that God was out ahead of me, preparing me to be a part of what he was doing at Hope before I arrived.

Colleen Fletcher, a member of the church staff, told me of a family in the church that would greatly appreciate a visit from me. That was in September. The family consisted of a father, a mother and a ten-year-old daughter. I remember her age because she was the age of my daughter. The father was dying of AIDS, having contracted the disease through a tainted blood transfusion. Colleen went with me to visit the family late one Sunday afternoon. I will call him Mike. At this point in the disease, he had become blind and could barely speak above a whisper. He sat on a sofa, propped up by pillows and as we entered the room smiled weakly as he waved a greeting with a bony hand. Fortunately his wife, who sat beside him, had not contracted the disease. I was touched and amazed at the warmth in their demeanor. She brought out tea and cookies, we chatted awhile, and not wanting to wear him out, I offered to pray before I left. But they urged me to stay a while longer. They had a vigorous faith, and their sense of humor actually sparkled. I could tell they were hoping I could come back for another visit before I left New Providence.

I said, "You guys know I'm leaving New Jersey for Hope College in December. But until I do, I'd love to come to visit each week on Sunday afternoon to pray with you and serve the Eucharist.

They eagerly accepted the offer. So, for the next many Sundays through the Autumn months, Colleen and I brought communion, read Scripture, talked about their lives and prayed with them. Occasionally their daughter would come into the room to welcome us and then go off to another room to watch television with her grandmother. I can still hear the distant mundane patter of that television when I remember those visits.

Then came the last visit, late in November. Over the weeks I had watched Mike deteriorate physically. His voice had become barely audible, his posture more and more drooped. But today his voice was strong, and he sat erect. His pale skin had a rosy tint.

I exclaimed, "Mike, you look great! What happened?" A bit of hyperbole, I admit, but appropriate.

He hesitated and said, "Oh, I guess it's because I'm taking more oxygen each day."

His wife said, "Mike, tell them what really happened."

After another pause, he told us the story. "One night this week I woke up and felt a presence in the room. Of course, I can't see, but I was sure someone was there in the room. It was an angel. Don't ask me to explain how I knew it was an angel. I just knew. And we had a conversation. At no point did I feel any fear, only peace. And he told me, 'I want you to tell your daughter that I will visit her after you die and that she shouldn't be afraid.' We talked about other things, but that was the main reason for his visit. While he was there, I felt a great surge of well-being and peace. I'm still feeling it. That's what you hear in my voice and see in my face."

What happened next is very hard to describe. As I listened to Mike, a great and glorious weight descended into the room, tremendous, but not oppressive or frightening. It was heavy and light, so heavy I couldn't move if I wanted to, and I didn't want to. I didn't feel crushed by the weight, but held. Enfolded in love. I thought of the Hebrew word *kabod*, translated "glory" in English, but meaning literally weight. It was a weight of glory, I believe. It was the presence of God. I knew everybody else in the room was feeling the same thing. So I said, "I think we need to be silent." And we were silent, for I don't know how long.

As we sat there, a sound rose up in my chest and into my throat. When it touched my tongue, I began to quietly speak something like a language, but unlike any language I had ever heard. It was barely a whisper, though audible, measured, distinct, oddly lyrical and utterly ecstatic. Utterly. I knew it was what I had heard called tongues or glossolalia. I also began to quietly weep, joyfully.

Before, when I thought about people I knew who testified of this experience, I thought of them as going over the edge of an emotional precipice, of losing control, of coming apart in a free fall of religious exuberance. But my experience was really the opposite: it was, as I said, an experience of being held, and embraced by God. In this sense I was losing control, willingly and happily, trading my control for Another's. I think of it as an emotional and experiential encounter with the reality Julian of Norwich wrote of: "enfolded in the Father, . . . enfolded in the Son, and . . . enfolded in the Holy Spirit . . . the Father . . . enfolded in us, and the Son . . . enfolded in us, and the Holy Spirit . . . enfolded in us: almightiness, all wisdom, all goodness: one God, one Lord."[43]

After a while, the "weight" lifted, and the "language" ceased. We looked at each other knowingly, but no one said a word. No one remarked, "What was that!?" I got up quietly, hugged Mike and his wife as I said goodbye and left with Colleen. All the while this was happening there was the distant sound of the television coming from another room. I'm not sure why it seemed important to me then, and still does. I have often wondered if hearing it was perhaps a way God anchored my heavenly, ecstatic experience in the normal.

I was grateful for the experience, though I didn't fully understand it. And I still don't. What I did come to understand in the next seven years of my assignment at Hope College, was how much I would need to be held and enfolded in God, and how deftly God in his providence had gone before me and prepared me for what was coming.

11

Joy Inexpressible
(Held in Love, part 2)

Though you have not seen him, you love him; and even though
you do not see him now, you believe in him and are filled
with an inexpressible and glorious joy.

—1 Peter 1:8

I didn't dream that an experience of quiet ecstasy in the home of a dying man in New Jersey, with the distant sound of a television droning in another room, would be so instrumental to my work at Hope College. I was held by divine love as I was moved in speech and powerful emotion. And the experience continued over the next seven years at Hope, in different ways, always quietly, with increasing frequency and often with tears.

It didn't mean that I got plugged into a direct pipeline to God, so I always knew exactly what to do. Instead of making me feel infallible, it made me feel safe; often confused and unsure, but somehow being nudged along, guided and loved by God, in spite of myself. So many times I managed to look smarter than I really was, finding myself in places and with people and situations I had no idea why, but which turned out to be perfect. Martin Luther wrote somewhere regarding his role in the Reformation, that he was like a man groping about in the dark in a church tower, reaching for something to steady himself, grabbing a rope that turned out to be the rope that rang the church bells. That was me at Hope College, muddling through, held by love, startled at what I saw happening. It was spiritually dazzling to believe that if I stumbled and fell, I would fall into God's arms.

The Vineyard Kids

This experience of being held in love surely opened the door for my relationship with the students from the Lakeshore Vineyard Church. The word got out that the new chapel dean spoke in tongues. Some students saw that as delightfully mind-blowing. Not that I advertised it as a sign that I belonged to that church, or that I always endorsed all of the manifestations of the Holy Spirit they celebrated. For instance, I was invited to be a guest at a midweek fellowship I believe they called a "Kinship Group." And I vividly remember feeling very uneasy as I saw several students laying on the floor, happily immobile, speaking in "tongues," "slain in the Spirit" as they termed it. But I didn't dismiss it as crazy either—a little bizarre maybe, but not sub-Christian. We were family. They were part of the flock I believed God had sent me to shepherd and gather. In the months ahead I saw the integrity and genuineness of their faith. And I came to see them behaving merely as one would expect some eighteen-to-twenty-two-year-olds to behave when held and moved by God's holy love—not fundamentally different from the way I behaved as a fifty-year-old.

The experience also opened a door with Darnisha Taylor. What an unexpected, extraordinarily talented gift she was, and still is to me personally. I started to say she was a sweet gift too, but that isn't quite the right word. If Darnisha was a flavor, she would be piquant, which is sweet without being saccharine, sweet with an attitude, pleasantly sharp and exciting, a woman of substance, to be reckoned with. When I met her, Darnisha was a recent Hope graduate, with a bachelor of arts degree in music, a black woman whose roots and experience as a Christian were in the Pentecostal church. In her undergraduate years she was only vaguely aware that there might be chapel services held in the chapel. She told me the only time she was in Dimnent Memorial Chapel was for senior music recitals. As she described her first experience as a student in the chapel, she said:

> I was from a Pentecostal background, so I was thinking, this is totally different for me, this whole environment. I remember coming in and opening one of the hymnals, and the organ began to play, which is beautiful. But I remember trying to read this incredibly complex music, and I was a music major. But how does anybody come and just enjoy this as worship? I was so perplexed, but it was right. There was about a handful of us in this gorgeous, huge auditorium, and I thought, Wow, okay, this isn't my experience in worship. But okay, got it.

After graduation she joined the admissions staff, and then the student development staff at the college with a focus on multicultural life. Given her background, forming a gospel choir seemed like a good multicultural programming idea. This went on for a while and the choir grew to forty students and everybody was happy. Meanwhile the revival was breaking out in chapel, and as she later described what she saw, "This is a whole 'nother level!" Looking back, it was inevitable that she and I would talk about the gospel choir becoming part of the chapel ministry. She remembered thinking in our first meeting,

> I was so surprised that Ben would be open to even inviting me to be a part of what was happening. . . . I know the background of this community and, I know I'm very different from it. Yeah, so I was blown away by how his heart was yes, this is awesome. Let's do it!

Our shared experience of the Holy Spirit opened the door that brought us together—she as a black Pentecostal rich in an unfettered expression of the gifts of the Spirit, and me as an awkward Reformed Church charismatic newbie. There was instant simpatico. Who'd have thought it? And I was about to see what I had seen in that prophetic dream on the north rim of the Grand Canyon, several months before—a black gospel choir rocking out in Dimnent Memorial Chapel, leading hundreds of students into the "white-hot enjoyment of God."[44] Once again, I got a glimpse of the divine choreographer at work in my life and ministry at Hope, dreams and all. Her efforts were hugely successful, enormously popular and profoundly significant for student worship. Darnisha recalls,

> Once the Lord plugged me into being a part of the chaplain's ministry, I remember starting by auditioning hundreds of students. By the end of my time here, I was auditioning four hundred students and had parents begging me, please start a second gospel choir. I started a second gospel choir, and it was just dynamic. We only had a room for 150 students, but it was such a special time of seeing what God was doing through the ministry and the revival that was happening. And you know, I can't take credit for that, but it was, it was . . . yeah!

Then there was the door that opened for Herm Kanis. I don't remember when or how he walked through that door into my life. It just seemed that one day he appeared like someone I had long been aware of in the corner of my eye, and knew before I knew him. There he was with his deep voice and twinkling eyes beneath bushy eyebrows, quick to laugh, playful and earnest, a Dutchman with no guile, offering to pray with me for the work at Hope. That was what we did for the larger part of the seven years I was dean of the chapel. He was also what I had newly come to call "of the charismatic persuasion." Our prayer times ebbed and flowed with glossolalia and ordinary speech as we interceded for the spiritual life of the college. Throughout, I was being held in love, especially when the conflict grew intense. He was a true friend in Christ—the answer to a prayer I had not prayed. And he bought me a lot of delicious lunches!

As much as I have benefited from these unique (for me!) visitations of the Holy Spirit, my theology of their place in the church is underdeveloped. But I'll tell you what I believe. I think the "tongues of fire" manifest on Pentecost in the book of Acts, when the gospel was preached in multiple languages, is a different thing than what I have experienced. And I don't believe that glossolalia is essential to authentic faith, or in any way a mark of advanced spirituality. My wife has never spoken in "tongues" but is as godly a person as I have ever met, and if the fruit of the Spirit is any measure of genuine spirituality, she is my superior in love, joy, peace, patience, kindness, goodness, faithfulness, gentleness, and self-control. All I know is that for me, spiritual tongues have been a way God has held me in his love, enfolded in the Father, the Son, and the Holy Spirit.

But why "tongues"? Why this odd speech that can sound like gibberish?

I can only speculate. Is it what Peter was thinking about when he assumed the embattled and persecuted churches in Asia Minor were experiencing a joy that was "inexpressible"? Did he mean that their joy went beyond reason and words and grammar and normal syntax? Or is it what Paul expressed when he prayed that the Ephesians would know what surpasses knowledge and experience the width, length, height, and depth of Christ's love?[45] Might a mere brush with the depths of God's beauty and holiness—experienced in some raw, elemental way which "no eye has seen, no ear has heard, no mind has conceived" (1 Corinthians 2:9)—leave one mute, or babbling and weeping?

Something like this appeared to have happened to Thomas Aquinas. One might say Aquinas was a man unusually skilled with words. His *Summa Theologica* is one of the greatest intellectual achievements of all time, attempting a unified view of all truth: art, science, literature, ethics, psychology, everything. It contains thirty-eight treatises, three thousand articles, and ten thousand objections. On December 6, 1273, after Thomas celebrated Mass in the chapel of St. Nicholas, he told his assistant Reginald of the vision of God he had while in worship, and the effect it had on him. He said,

I can do no more; such things have been revealed to me that all I have written seems to me as so much straw. Now I await the end of my life, and after that the end of my works.

And he wrote no more until his death shortly thereafter.

Why the tears? I cry almost every time I talk about inexpressible joy. A conversation with Ben Patterson on joy can be time-consuming! Why should joy have any tears at all? I think it is because, as Frederick Buechner suggests, "the marvelous and impossible thing truly happens."[46] Tears well up from that place deep within where guilt and grace, human misery and divine love meet. At its deepest, joy springs from the realization that things need not have been so good, in fact should not have, but are. The inevitable is overtaken by the unforeseeable, mercy triumphs over judgment, and joy breaks in, "beyond the walls of the world, poignant as grief."[47] Tears of grief and tears of joy flow from very nearly the same place, and "those who sow in tears will reap with songs of joy" (Psalm 126:5). Harvests are usually messy.

Charles Spurgeon once prayed that God would send his congregation a season of "holy disorder." He wanted the worthless and lesser things to be shaken up and swept away, so the deck could be cleared to make room for God's fresh blessings. Augustine prayed a similar prayer:

How shall I call upon my God, my God and my Lord, since, in truth, when I call upon him, I call him into myself? What place is there within me where my God can come? How can God come into me, God, who made heaven and earth? O Lord my God, is there anything in me that can contain you?[48]

The answer is no, nothing in us can contain him. Something must happen to us, something radical. We must somehow be increased. For God to come in, God must make room for God. Some things may have to be swept aside so the really wonderful thing may come in. It may be messy, even painful to be expanded in our desires and capacities, but remember, the wonderful thing is God and his joy.

So when we prayed for spiritual revival to come to Hope, we were praying to be held in love by the Holy Spirit, the Holy Disorderer.

12

With Christ in the School of Prayer

"If you want to know what people really believe," the philosopher Roger Scruton once explained, "listen to them pray." It is one thing to ask a person what he believes, but it is another thing to listen to him pray. Prayers reveal the underlying theology. As the old Latin formula reminds us, Lex Orandi, Lex Credendi—As we pray, so we believe.

—Albert Mohler

You can do more than pray after you have prayed, but you can never do more than pray until you have prayed.

—A. J. Gordon

That night I described earlier at Forest Home, in 1962,[49] Dr. Orr said two things in his lecture about revival that have reverberated in my spirit ever since. One was about the mystery and necessity of earnest prayer in spiritual awakening. The other was about repentance. The two go together.

I'll start with prayer.

Orr confessed that he didn't understand how prayer works, just that the Lord commands it. I didn't understand it either. He wondered especially how God's sovereign will interacts with human freedom and petition. And so did I. How is it that a God who can do anything chooses not to do some things until we ask? Even plead? "All I know," he said, "is that whenever God wants to do something, he sets his people to praying." His lecture showed that earnest prayer, that mysterious necessity, has been at the heart of every spiritual awakening in history. I left that meeting determined to pray that way for revival in the church and on my campus.

It should not have surprised me that my will and capacity for prayer was to be tested immediately.

I came down the mountain (a statement loaded with biblical resonances!) determined to dive into the necessity and mystery of intercessory prayer. I told my friends what I had heard about spiritual awakenings, and proposed that we do the same thing that students had done in the spiritual awakenings of the past. To get started, we eagerly determined to pray two hours for the salvation of the unconverted high school students we were working with. We purposed to storm heaven and bring down the blessings of God for these kids. One of us had a part time job in a church, so he asked the pastor if we could meet for prayer in the church building, a logical place to pray, one would think. The pastor told us to just show up on any evening of our choosing. Since my friend had a key to the building, we could pray anywhere we wanted. But the night we came by to pray, the church was bustling with activity, as various committee meetings, youth programs, and a choir practice were spread throughout the facility. The church building was busier and more full of distraction than our homes and dorm rooms. The only free space was a large janitor's closet that smelled strongly of detergent and disinfectant.

So we gathered in that closet to pour out our hearts before God. We had two hours to do nothing but stand before the throne of God and plead for the salvation of souls. We prayed every which way we could think of: we praised God and confessed our sins and lifted up the names of every student we knew. Then we praised and confessed and interceded some more. When we had prayed for everything and everyone in every way imaginable, over and over, I looked at my watch to see if we had any time left. Just fifteen minutes had passed! The next one hour and forty-five minutes of prayer were the longest and slowest I had ever experienced. When I came to pour out my heart before God, I found that there wasn't much there to pour out.

It was clear that I had a lot to learn about prayer. But I had much more to learn about the repentance necessary to pray—especially repentance.

It was the 1960s.

The tumultuous decade of the '60s was just beginning, and I had no idea how thoroughly my passion for prayer and revival would be leached out of me before it was over. I say this with deep regret. I can sum up those years of my life with the title of Malcolm Muggeridge's autobiography, *Chronicles of Wasted Time*. The academic study of religion, the emergence of psychology and sociology as alternative faiths, and my work in the mainline church—none of these were friendly to the vision of my naive youth. If my seminary experience taught me anything about prayer, it was its irrelevance, judging from its total neglect in the life of the seminary curriculum and community. Intellectual pride, religious professionalism, and the hubris of what would become the most narcissistic era in American history, conspired to damage my soul.

Also, during that season, I took an extended journey into the "far country" morally and spiritually.

I emerged from the '60s angry, jaded, and full of hubris. Like so many of that generation, I was captivated by the idea of systemic or institutional evil. I saw it everywhere: in politics, business, education, and religion—especially religion. Where my earlier piety saw the evil of institutions as the evil of the human heart writ large, my secularized piety tended to blame the institutions for doing most of the writing. Fix the institutions, and you'll fix a lot of what's wrong with humans. My institutional field was the church. The church was pretty screwed up, I thought—thus, my anger. And I knew just what it needed: it needed me and my new insights—thus, my hubris. If I could only get my hands on the church for a while, I could fix it.

I had a group of friends who shared my anger toward the church, my chutzpah and sense of humor. That got me involved with them in publishing a satirical magazine named *The Wittenburg Door*.[50] The quality of the publication was uneven, but I probably wouldn't be a writer today if I hadn't been involved with them. It also fed my temerity and sharpened my pleasure in speaking truth to power and the ridiculous. The name *Wittenburg Door* was an allusion to the Ninety-Five Theses Luther nailed to the Wittenburg church door in Germany, protesting the abuses of the sixteenth-century church. We kind of saw ourselves as doing something like that. More chutzpah, I guess.

A scholar pointed out that we had misspelled Wittenberg, using the letter u, instead of the letter e in berg. It didn't bother us.

Our planning meetings were monthly breakfasts at Hob Nob Hill in San Diego. We'd eat, crack jokes, complain about the silly and stupid things we saw in evangelicalism, and generally blow off steam for a couple of hours. Someone would take notes on all the gesticulation and blather and then assign articles for us to write for the next Door issue. It was great fun. The note taker was Denny Rydberg, who later became president of Young Life.

However, as Oscar Wilde wrote, "There are only two tragedies in life: one is not getting what one wants, and the other is getting it." I was about to suffer both calamities. *If I could just get my hands on the church for a while, I could fix it.* And so in 1975, God gave me what I wanted: he called me to start a new church in Irvine, California. I was elated. I could start from the ground floor without the mistakes of unenlightened predecessors to cramp my creativity. I knew it wouldn't be easy. I was more than a little scared at the prospect, but I believed this thing could be done! With God's help, of course, and the help of friends with like vision, it could happen! We could build a church that would be the pinnacle to which two thousand years of Christian history had struggled to reach.

It took nearly seven years for me to lose confidence in myself. It came by way of two bulging disks in the lumbar region of my back. If I ever wondered whether C. S. Lewis was right about pain being "God's megaphone" that experience settled the argument. The doctor had prescribed six weeks of total rest, just to determine whether surgery was needed. My first thought was *OK, I guess I'll get a lot of reading done*. But due to the pain, the painkillers, the muscle relaxants, and lying on my back, my eyes didn't focus well. I read one book in six weeks. And I couldn't lie in bed either; it was too soft. So the six weeks were spent on the floor. The pain was horrible and humiliating. A trip to the bathroom was a race between my bladder and my capacity for pain. Sometimes I had to lie down on the bathroom floor to recover from the trip before I could do what the trip was for.

"When You're Well You Think You're in Charge"

I was of no use to the church, so I thought. I couldn't preach and devise imaginative programs, I couldn't lead meetings, I couldn't make calls. I couldn't do anything but pray. So I asked my wife, Lauretta, to bring me the new church directory with the pictures of all the church members in it. I decided I would pray for every member every day I was on the floor. It took nearly two hours for me to do this. Don't misunderstand: this was not great piety. Mainly I was bored and frustrated. But very quickly those times of prayer became sweet.

Toward the end of my convalescence, I went for a walk and was back on the floor resting and thinking about going back to work. I said to the Lord, "You know, these times of prayer have been sweet. It's too bad I won't have time to do this when I'm at work." Then the Lord spoke. "Stupid," was how he addressed me. That was his word. He said it in a friendly tone of voice though. He said, "Stupid, You have the same twenty-four hours each day when you're well as when you're sick. The trouble with you, Ben, is when you're well you think you're in charge; when you're sick, you know you're not."

He was right, of course. That led me to consider how well I had been doing when I was "in charge." The church I had hoped would be special, set apart, a city set on a hill, an army beating down the gates of hell, a model for other churches to pattern themselves after, was turning out like all the others. By God's mercy it was a good church. The people were precious. Jesus loves his church. But it wasn't special—or at least any more special than any number of other flawed churches. Every mistake I ever swore I'd never make as a pastor I had made by then and then some. Everything I swore would never happen in my church had happened by then and then some. And most important: the world was still going to hell, and we appeared to be impotent to do anything about it.

In many ways we were no different from the rest of the churches in North America. We had an abundance of resources. By any international standard, we were rich in education, land, money, media, technology, and programs. But was the city of Irvine appreciably different because we and the other churches were in town? Not much, it seemed.

I was hopeless; I had lost confidence in what I thought I was capable of. But it was a benign hopelessness, the negative side of repentance. The positive side was that I was learning to pray again, *wanting* to pray again because I had hope! My hands were empty and I wanted God to fill them with the things that only he can give and that he promises to give to those who persist in asking, seeking, and knocking (Luke 11:9–10). My church was just a little flock, and I was just a little pastor, unequal to the task of building the kingdom of God. But it was to the little ones that Jesus said, "Do not be afraid, little flock, for your Father has been pleased to give you the kingdom" (Luke 12:32). I was deathly exhausted from trying to build the church *for* Jesus. I was in way over my head. It was way too hard, and I was failing. At its deepest, my repentance was wanting to learn to build the church *with* Jesus. After all, Jesus said he is the one who builds his church (Matthew 16:18), and "Unless the LORD builds the house, its builders labor in vain (Psalm 127:1). Kingdom building begins in communion with the Master Builder; and it is sustained and completed in communion with Jesus. That's prayer. That's *with* Jesus. That's why Peter Taylor Forsyth declared that "the worst sin is prayerlessness . . . and not to want to pray, then, is the sin behind sin."[51] The reason is simple: God is God and we are not. Not to pray is to act as though we don't need God, or worse, think we are God. Prayerlessness is practical atheism.

Chastened and renewed, when I came to Hope I asked my staff to commit to doing everything, *everything* with prayer, by prayer, and through prayer. Our routine was to pray together for an hour before each of the four chapel services each week. Not only that, we periodically spent whole days in prayer throughout the year.

Why did we pray so much? In large part because we felt so keenly our weakness. We felt the sting of opposition and suspicion among significant portions of the faculty, and the inertia of the historic indifference of Hope students to chapel. We knew we were in over our heads. We knew we needed the Lord.

But in larger part we prayed because we believed prayer was an act of spiritual realism. The real battle, the ultimate struggle is in the realm of the unseen, not with opponents and attitudes accessible to our five senses. The apostle Paul describes our combat equipment is utterly otherworldly: things like the helmet of salvation, the belt of truth and the breastplate of righteousness, the shield of faith and the sword of the Spirit which is the word of God. How on earth are we to put on those otherworldly things? The apostle says by "praying at all times in the Spirit" (Ephesians 6:18 ESV). We fight the good fight by prayer, because God is the armor. Literally, as David prayed, "you are a shield around me, O LORD" (Psalm 3:3).

Praying so much took a lot of time. Our days were full of meetings with students and the constant pressure of planning four chapel services a week. That amounted to more than a hundred meetings a year. But we took our cue from Martin Luther, who said the busier he got the more he felt he needed to pray. We believed that if we were too busy to pray, then we were too busy, fatally too busy. It was that simple.

Dolores Nasrallah was intrigued by all this prayer stuff, and a little puzzled. She had just finished seminary and came out of a very successful church ministry with a lot of great ideas about creative programming. At first she asked me when we were going to get around to doing some of those wonderful programs. We did get around to it later, a little bit, but mainly we prayed. Later she told me in a personal letter,

> Those prayer times were pivotal. They were holy ground to me. We shared God sightings.[52] We confessed sins. We worshipped God.... We listened to God in stillness and quiet as a community. Then we talked about what we heard the Holy Spirit tell us, and we often even changed course for the subsequent service minutes away as a result of what we heard. Listening prayer in community is something I have never experienced before or since, and I must say, I miss it greatly! Thank you for modeling that for me. I think it is worth

mentioning it, because it was a result of those prayers that our faith grew, we believed, and the revival came. God moved in a big way in answer to our prayers.

Her words echoed the experience of the entire campus ministries staff. For all of us, prayer was a thrilling, sometime even scary experiment in the mystery of "what if." What if we really acted as though God was in charge and we were not? It was actually fun.

"The Ultimate Interference with the Status Quo"

I said at the beginning of chapter 9 that I wanted to avoid open conflict as long as I could. The truth, however, is that prayer is not escape from conflict. Prayer is direct engagement with the enemy. It is stealth warfare. No one may see us pray, but the devil does, and the devil hates it when we pray. Theologian David Wells calls prayer "the ultimate interference with the status quo."[53] We pray because we are spiritual realists. We are at war with the powers of darkness.

A delightful irony emerged as we prayed. By avoiding, or at least postponing open conflict, we engaged in a deeper, more radical conflict. And we learned that there is more than one way to pray—that our prayers weren't confined to what we did in the privacy of our staff meetings; they were also what we did publicly with the hundreds of students who came to the chapel services. Vigorous, powerful, exuberant prayers were prayed *when we sang together*.

13

"Those Who Sing Pray Twice"

*Through the praise of children and infants you have established
a stronghold.*

—Psalm 8:2

*Jehoshaphat appointed men to sing to the LORD and to praise him for the
splendor of his holiness as they went out at the head of the army, saying:
"Give thanks to the LORD, for his love endures forever."*

—2 Chronicles 20:21

*May the praise of God be in their mouths and a
double-edged sword in their hands.*

—Psalm 149:6

Let all the world in every corner sing.

—George Herbert

Something quietly earthshaking and transformative seemed to happen in one of our earliest chapel services. After we sang a particular song, I sensed that some *thing,* something dark and malevolent, had actually fled Dimnent Memorial Chapel.

I am suspicious of anyone who makes that kind of claim—that simply because they felt something happen in a sanctuary or anywhere, something invisible and beyond sense, something evil, that it must have actually happened. In fact, I am predisposed to scoff at those kinds of declarations, and the people that make them. But that experience, and others like it, among other members of my staff, was so vivid that it set us to reflecting biblically on our singing. We talked a lot about the power of sung praise, especially in the spiritual conflict we found ourselves in. What follows are some of the convictions and insights that emerged over the next seven years.

General Dwight

The story of King Jehoshaphat in 2 Chronicles 20 seemed to jump off the page when we read it together, because it embodied what we believed the Holy Spirit was doing when we sang in chapel. And it amused us to no end. Jehoshaphat was the king of Judah when a national crisis—one of many—shook the nation. An international alliance of large armies were poised to invade and overwhelm little Judah. So King Jehoshaphat led the people in a desperate prayer for God's help. As he prayed, terrified men and women and their children stood there with him, trembling before the Lord. The prayer ended with,

O our God, will you not judge [our enemies]? For we have no power to face this vast army that is attacking us. We do not know what to do, but our eyes are upon you. (2 Chronicles 20:12)

The Lord answered their prayer. They were so confident he would scatter their enemies, that when their army went out to fight them, they were led by a choir—a choir!—of Levites, at the head of the army. Singers would be their weapon, because though invisible, the Lord and his heavenly hosts were the army. As they marched into battle the choir praised the Lord "for the splendor of his holiness . . . , saying: 'Give thanks to the LORD, for his love endures forever'" (2 Chronicles 20:21).

Can you imagine what the enemy armies thought when they saw the little army of Judah charging into battle behind a choir? No officers, only bass, baritone, and tenor singers. No need to imagine, for the enemy armies were dead when Judah's army arrived. Every last soldier was a corpse. The battle belonged to the Lord, as all battles do.

In the spirit of Jehoshaphat, we playfully started calling Dwight Beal, our director of music and worship, "General Dwight." One day, a few years into his ministry, we laid hands on him and commissioned him in seriousness as "General Dwight." Why not? He and the student worship teams he trained so well had been leading us with great authority and skill in the singing part of our chapel worship services. The title was never made official, but it was descriptive of the significance of his work in the Hope College revival.

"Those Who Sing Pray Twice"

Psalm 8 also came to stand out in my thinking. This biblical prayer—which being a psalm, is also a song—was written to be sung in public worship. It celebrates God's glory in creation, and declares the powerful and authoritative role humans play, even young, and otherwise clueless little humans, to establish his sovereign rule. All of this, simply by praise.

You have taught children and infants to tell of your strength, silencing your enemies and all who oppose you. (Psalm 8:2 NLT)

Jesus quoted this very line from Psalm 8 to silence his critics when he entered Jerusalem the week before he was crucified. The "authorities," the chief priests and teachers of the law, complained that children were shouting Jesus's praise as he entered the city, and demanded that he stop the kids. But he shot back, quoting this prayer-song, and saying in effect, "Haven't you read that children's praise is an assault on God's enemies, which in this case is . . . you? You people are the 'foe and the aggressor' of the psalm."[54]

Psalm 8 declares songs of praise to be war songs, battle cries, effectual prayers of combat that actually silence God's enemies, even the most powerful and shrewd, and even when prayed by the weak and unsophisticated. This is nothing less than ridiculous from the world's perspective. Eugene Peterson understood this when he translated Psalm 8:4 (The Message):

Nursing infants gurgle choruses about you; toddlers shout the songs That drown out enemy talk, and silence atheist babble.

I still smile to myself when I pray this psalm, and think of the prayers we prayed during those years, as we sang corporately in Dimnent Memorial Chapel. Not all of our songs were polished hymnody, to say the least. But they were genuine praise and genuinely detestable and terrifying to dark powers. This is by no means to deny the value of traditional music and lyrical excellence, or to imply that people who didn't like the things we sang belonged to the dark powers. God is honored by thoughtful and artistic virtuosity. But it is to suggest that these things can be overrated among certain aesthetes, and especially in institutions of higher learning, to the neglect of the spiritual impact of a song.

Doors flew open in my mind when I saw the warlike nature of sung praise. The sung praise of God by children and infants was holy war against God's enemies. The psalms, the longest book in the Bible, is a prayer book, and all its prayers are songs! On the most fundamental, organic level, the link between praying and singing is indissoluble. A psalm is a song is a prayer.

The famous quote attributed to St. Augustine came to mind: "Those who sing pray twice." Actually, this sentence cannot be found anywhere in Augustine's writings, so no one knows who actually said it. But no matter, because it's true—gloriously true. All our singing in chapel was prayer—uproarious, joyous spiritual warfare in Dimnent Memorial Chapel.

"Singing Like a Black Lady"

I think I was discovering this truth before I knew I was discovering it. In the last church I pastored before coming to Hope, I traveled to Jamaica Queens, New York City, to preach in a friend's church: Bishop Roderick Caesar's wonderful Pentecostal congregation, the Bethel Gospel Tabernacle. Most of his people were African Americans of Caribbean descent. My seven-year-old daughter Mary was with us, and she was very impressed by what she saw and heard. She listened carefully as these godly Christians shared their prayer concerns with each other. Jamaica Queens can be a dangerous place to raise children, so many of their prayers were for their protection from the violence of gangs and guns and drugs at school. Her eyes grew big and she became very still as she listened. Then she participated in a joyous service of song—and dance!—quite unlike anything she had ever seen as the child of a Presbyterian pastor.

A few weeks later, my wife, Lauretta, came home a little late one afternoon, fifteen minutes after Mary was to be home from school. As Lauretta walked up to the door she heard Mary inside, singing loudly and boisterously. It sounded like a seven-year-old white girl's version of what she remembered hearing at Bethel Gospel Tabernacle. When Lauretta opened the door, Mary whirled around, ran to her Mom and hugged her. She had been scared to be home alone, she said. The lower level of our split-level house was especially frightening to her. It was dark down in the lower level, and who knew what evil might be lurking in the shadows? So she stood at the top of the steps going down to the lower level and sang into the darkness. Lauretta asked her why she sang in that particular style. Mary answered, "I was scared, so I started singing like a black lady!"

She had learned something that Sunday in Jamaica Queens, New York, that I hope she will carry with her the rest of her life. When the present is terrifying, she can sing defiantly into the darkness like those valiant women in Jamaica Queens, because the praise of God silences and actually terrifies our "enemies and all who oppose" us. The people of Bethel Gospel Tabernacle weren't singing as they did in spite of the perils of the city. They were singing because of the dangers. Exuberant praise and worship were the weapons of their warfare.

By Stealth

Are you wondering what was the song/prayer we sang when I felt something evil leave the chapel? It was a song we sang over and over again our first year. Prominent among its lyrics was:

One name under heaven

Whereby we must be saved,

One name under heaven

Whereby we must be saved. . . .

God's gonna move this place

God's gonna move this place

God's gonna turn this place upside down. By that . . .

One name under heaven

Whereby we must be saved.[55]

The supremacy of Christ, and the exclusivity of the gospel message had long been diminished at Hope, ignored and even denied, on multiple levels of the college community. Spiritual torpor and indifference had permeated much of the student body. "Other" gospels, substitute gospels, were gaining ascendancy. Christians who in another time and place would be regarded simply as orthodox believers were routinely sneered at as "fundamentalist," narrow-minded bigots, and obscurantist. Increasingly, in some of the academic centers of the college, the idea of Christian missions to Muslims and other false religions was eviscerated to no more than social services and interreligious dialogue, insipid efforts to help Muslims become better Muslims. The name of Samuel Zwemer, the college's distinguished missionary alumnus, the "Apostle to Islam" was nowhere to be found on the campus. In one academic department his work was dismissed as misguided and irrelevant.

Singing songs like "One Name" in such an environment of apostasy and indifference might have looked and sounded harmless. But it was a raw encounter with deception, a holy war. And God was moving this place by stealth, by means the world considers innocuous—by prayer and praise.

But it wasn't entirely by stealth. There was one thing we did that was public and potentially (usually, often) offensive.

We preached and taught. Those who sing pray twice . . . and preach.

14

This Is Not My Opinion

There is something definite in the Bible. . . . Believing, therefore, that there is such a thing as truth, and such a thing as falsehood, that there are truths in the Bible, and the gospel consists in something definite which is to be believed by men, it becomes us to be decided as to what we teach, and to teach it in a decided manner. We are to deal with men who will be either lost or saved, and they certainly will not be saved by erroneous doctrine. We have to deal with God, whose servants we are, and he will not be honored by our delivering falsehoods; neither will he give us a reward and say, "Well done, good and faithful servant, thou hast mangled the gospel as judiciously as any man that ever lived before thee."

—Charles Haddon Spurgeon

Those who do not love the truth excuse themselves on the grounds that it is disputed and that very many people deny it. Thus their error is solely due to the fact that they love neither the truth nor charity, and so they have no excuse.

—Pascal

A Hope College professor said to me,

We really don't like it when you preach and say, "This is the Word of God." We wouldn't mind what you preached, if you just said, "This is my opinion. There are other opinions, but I would like you to listen to mine now." But what you always say is, "Thus says the Lord." That's what makes us so angry.

Those words are pretty much exactly what he said. Specifically when he said, "If you just said, 'This is my opinion. There are other opinions, but I would like you to listen to mine now,'" it so struck me that I wrote it down immediately after our conversation to make sure I remembered it correctly.

I think the professor who said this was genuinely trying to be helpful. He was trying to explain and assuage the animosity he believed so many of his colleagues on the Hope faculty had toward me and my preaching.

Exactly how many of these people there actually were was never clear. They may have been just a few, their voices louder than their numbers. Whatever the case, it felt wrong.

So I tried to imagine preaching that way.

I imagined standing before the pulpit in Dimnent Memorial Chapel and announcing before more than a thousand students gathered to hear the sermon, "My text is John 14:6:"

> Jesus answered, "I am the way and the truth and the life. No one comes to the Father except through me."

Then suppose I declared after reading it, "This is the Word of God," and they solemnly answered in the words of the ancient litany, "Thanks be to God."

Then suppose I began to preach this classic magisterial text, which we had just declared to be the Word of God, by saying, "What I am about to say is just my opinion. There are other opinions, but I would like you to listen to mine now."

That proposed scenario was more than insipid. It was appalling. I simply could not say that what I preached was merely my opinion. And not because of what I believed about my words. It was because of what I believed about the Bible's words—what has been termed the perspicuity of Scripture. I believed that God's Word in the Bible is sufficiently clear to be understood and declared authoritatively with human words by mere mortals, whether spoken by Augustine or Aquinas, John Chrysostom or John Calvin, Billy Sunday or Billy Graham or any number of preachers throughout Christian history, heralded and unheralded. There are murky and controversial passages here and there that defy understanding or agreement. But they are the exception, are few in number, and never contrary to the central message of the Bible. With all its mysteries and puzzles, the Bible was written to be understood, meditated on, and taught.

Sweltering through My Ordination

More to the point, what I tried to preach was rooted in a deep and ancient tradition, not Ben Patterson's private perspectives and reflections. I believed, and still believe, there really is something that C. S. Lewis called "Mere Christianity"—an identifiable body of belief that has been embraced by Christians of a variety of historical traditions spanning two thousand years. Or as Vincent of Lerins (d. 445) put it, there are certain things in Christianity that have been believed, "everywhere, always and by all." I wanted my beliefs and my preaching to be united with those folks in a fellowship based on biblical authority and orthodoxy, the historic creeds, the Nicene doctrine of the Trinity, and the deity of Christ. I was constantly judging what I preached and taught by that great tradition. I strove to preach within what the Apostle's Creed calls the "communion of saints."

This holy mandate was imprinted in my soul on a warm, muggy night in La Jolla, California, May 1975.[56] This was the night I sweltered through my ordination into the ministry of the Word and the sacraments. Throughout the service I heard Scripture read, a sermon preached and a charge given to remind me of the great responsibilities I was taking on as a pastor and preacher. I'm not sure which made me sweat more: the responsibilities I was contemplating or the weather.

At the end of the service I was asked to kneel before the congregation as the church's elders laid their hands on my shoulders to set me apart for this great work and prayed that I have the strength to do it. This was very difficult for me physically. I was soaked in sweat, the heat and humidity of the evening exacerbated by the heavy Genevan robe I was wearing. I have a gimpy left knee from an old football injury that made kneeling painful, and the elders hands on my shoulders were exceedingly heavy. Just two hands would be light, but there were about twenty people wanting to lay their hands on my shoulders, and the weight of their collective hands was pushing me down into the thick carpet in the front of the church. Everybody wanted to pray for me! Everybody must have thought I was really going to need prayer. It went on and on and on, as prayer after prayer was prayed. My legs started to cramp, and my back to ache from the pressure. Even my breathing was labored. I was on the edge of desperation, and about to stand up and shout "Amen, already!"

But I was exactly where I needed to be to hear the closing prayer, prayed by the pastor. He prayed, "Lord, as Ben feels the weight of these hands on his shoulders,"—oh how I felt the weight!—"may he also feel the weight of the sacred responsibility he is taking on to speak and to serve faithfully in your name." I felt it, I really felt it! Then he prayed a prayer that has sustained me through my entire ministry:

May he also feel the strength of your everlasting arms holding and empowering him to do the work.

When Mere Is More [57]

I have always felt the weight of what I am called to do, and the need of God's strength and wisdom to do it rightly—except when I haven't, Lord have mercy! Who am I, I often wonder, as I stand before a crowd to preach the Word of God and to tell them what God Almighty thinks? I acutely fear that I may misrepresent the Lord by speaking falsehood in his name. I equally fear not speaking with the conviction, unction, and earnestness appropriate to proclaiming his Word.

The tradition I am most closely aligned with is Protestant and evangelical. But it is rooted in the deeper soil of Mere Christianity. That is the larger reality. I believe this tradition broadens my mind and nurtures in me an ecumenical spirit that unites me with Christians across the traditions and the centuries. Our unity is based not on a lowest common denominator—the latest fads, revisions, and heresies of the last few decades—but the highest common denominator, a body of doctrine, objectively true, once for all given by God to the church to preserve, defend, and proclaim. As C. S. Lewis wrote:

> "Measured against the ages, 'mere Christianity' turns out to be no insipid interdenominational transparency, but something positive, self-consistent, and inexhaustible. . . . Despite all the divisions, [there] still appears . . . an immensely formidable unity. . . . For you have now got on to the great level viaduct which crosses the ages and which looks so high from the valleys, so low from the mountains, so narrow compared with the swamps, and so broad compared with the sheep tracks."[58]

During my years at Hope, this vision and imperative was fed by a periodical I continue to read. The title says it all: Touchstone: A Journal of Mere Christianity. A "touchstone" is a criterion or a benchmark—the benchmark being what Christians have believed in all times and places. Touchstone's editorial board, writers, and readership include Christians who are members of Anglican, Baptist, Eastern Orthodox, Lutheran, Methodist, Presbyterian, Roman Catholic, and many other churches. They don't soft-pedal their differences, but when they argue, they argue as members of one family, the holy church.

Old Truths, Double Distilled

So of course, when I preached the Bible at Hope, I was compelled to preach as one who believes he is preaching the truth, not my truth, but *the* truth, God's truth—exuberantly and fiercely. Being both human and a sinner, I no doubt did not always get it right, and my tone may not always have been gracious, but the tradition of Mere Christianity, of the things believers have held to "everywhere, always and by all," kept me from wandering too far from the truth. To have preached it timidly, to offer it as one man's somewhat tentative opinion on religious matters would dishonor the Bible, and the God who inspired the Bible. Moreover, since the truth of the gospel is a matter of life and death, it must be preached with the intensity and conviction proper to matters of life and death.

E. M. Bounds, that fiery man of prayer from the nineteenth century, explains most clearly why I could not say, "This is my opinion," when I preached:

> It is not new truth that the world needs, so much as the constant iteration of old truths, yet ever new truths, of the Bible . . . double distilled.[59]

This conviction was fed by the story of a great twentieth century evangelist, Billy Graham.

Forest Home, where I met Ray Smith, and worked for seven summers, was a place profoundly affected by what happened to evangelist Billy Graham when he visited the conference center in the summer of 1949. That was before Billy Graham became BILLY GRAHAM, the evangelist who, over the next half century, preached the gospel in massive stadium events, on the radio, and on television to untold millions worldwide, and whose ministry included counseling presidents and kings. More people heard the gospel from Billy Graham than any one person in history.

A Major Bridge Was Crossed

But in 1949 he was in his early thirties, confused and dispirited, with more questions than answers about a faith he wasn't sure he even believed anymore. He was so discouraged, he even considered going back to work as a dairy farmer in North Carolina. His doubts were fed by the defection of his close friend Charles Templeton, who had been an evangelist with Billy with Youth for Christ in the 1940s. Templeton had left the faith he and Billy shared, announcing himself to be an agnostic after attending Princeton Seminary. He often chided Graham for his naive faith in the Bible.

So when Henrietta Mears, the director of Forest Home, invited Graham to preach at the conference center in August of 1949, he accepted with tremendous misgivings. To make his uncertainty more distressing, he had also scheduled an evangelistic outreach in Los Angeles in September.

One night, as he wandered through the woods at Forest Home, praying in anguish, his spiritual crisis came to a head. As he tells it in his autobiography, he fell to his knees and prayed,

> O God! There are many things in this book I do not understand. There are many problems with it for which I have no solution. There are many seeming contradictions. There are some areas in it that do not seem to correlate with modern science. I can't answer some of the philosophical and psychological questions Chuck (Charles Templeton) and others are raising. . . . [But] Father, I am going to accept this as Thy Word—by *faith*! I am going to allow faith to go beyond my intellectual questions and doubts, and I will believe this to be Your inspired Word![60]

When he stood up, tears stung his eyes, but he felt the power and presence of God in a way he hadn't in months. "A major bridge had been crossed," he said. The next day he preached at Forest Home and four hundred people made a commitment to Christ.

A few weeks later, the historic Los Angeles outreach began in a tent erected on the corner of Washington and Hill Streets. It was scheduled to last three weeks, but stretched to eight weeks in the "Canvas Cathedral" as the newspapers dubbed it. Media outlets nationwide began talking about Billy Graham, and the rest, as they say, is history. I have heard Graham preach many times, and the phrase he used repeatedly for the rest of his ministry was "the Bible says."

Graham's story is memorialized today on a plaque beside Lake Mears at Forest Home. But before the plaque was even placed there, we all knew roughly where the spot was—the spot by the lake where his momentous and history-making decision was made. Most of the seven summers I worked there, first as a collegian, later as a seminary student, I led a fitness and leadership training program for high school boys. That meant I got up every morning at five o'clock in the high altitude, and ran with my teenage charges up to the lake for rigorous calisthenics and a "polar bear" swim. A lot of joyful physical exertion and youthful male camaraderie took place across the lake from the Billy Graham memorial.

I rarely thought about it, but I can see now how I unconsciously acquired a physical, emotional, and spiritual connection with Forest Home and Graham's commitment to preach the Bible as God's Word. In the seven summers I spent at Forest Home, my mind and spirit were "marinated" not only in his story, but in the faithful souls who shared his convictions. Their passion became my passion. There were other influences, but his night of decision in 1949 has been sealed in my soul as an icon of what I've wanted to be. And it has held me even when I wanted to abandon it as Graham was once tempted. On any particular occasion my interpretation of a text of Scripture may have been flawed. But it would be a sin to preach the Bible tentatively.

An Argument about Furniture

In one sense my argument, with the professor who wanted me to frame my sermons as opinion pieces, was an argument about furniture. If there is an item of furniture that symbolizes much of academic life and culture it is a round table—a place where equals, both colleagues and scholars, meet for conversation, to discuss, argue, and banter ideas.

Round tables tend toward the approximate and open ended.

But a pulpit, on the other hand, is the furniture of declaration and pronouncement, of teaching, authority, command, and exhortation.

Between the two there is always the potentiality, if not the inevitability of conflict. A round table requires a moderator, a pulpit requires a preacher. The two will always clash.

My pulpit was the Holy Scriptures, the ancient faith, mere Christianity, the Vincentian Canon. When I stood at the pulpit, I did not merely stand for the faith, I knelt before the faith, accountable to the triune God, "the glorious company of Apostles, the noble fellowship of the prophets, and the white robed army of martyrs." Whatever academic freedom might mean to the Hope College community, my deepest conviction was that I was born not to be free to think whatever I wanted to think, but to adore and serve the truth.

The pressing question is: what is the acceptable scope of theological diversity in a Christian community? When does ecumenical become heretical? Merely Christian, vaguely Christian?

My driving conviction was, and still is, that there are some things a Christian college should no longer debate—as though they were still open questions—things like the deity and uniqueness of Christ and the sinfulness of practicing homosexuality. It is fine and desirable to discuss all other options to Christian truth in a classroom—but in the context of a community publicly committed to the truth, and led by professors who profess and firmly adhere to the historic faith.

15

God-Breathed

*All Scripture is God-breathed and is useful for teaching, rebuking, correcting
and training in righteousness, so that the servant of God may be
thoroughly equipped for every good work.*
—2 Timothy 3:16–17

What were you thinking?

It wasn't the first time I had promised to do something I later regretted. But none of the other times had been so scary. As I paced nervously in the room next to the church sanctuary, I was chastising myself: *What were you thinking? Why did you agree to do this?*

What I had agreed to do was recite from memory, before a large crowd, the entire book of Revelation in the Bible. I would do it with two other men: Bill Brownson, a retired Words of Hope radio minister, and Tim Brown, a professor at Western Theological Seminary. It was Bill who talked Tim and me into doing this crazy thing. Part of his "pitch" was that he had done it many times before, and had seen God bless it powerfully. Now he was getting old and probably wouldn't be able to do it much longer. His appeal was, would you younger men please do this as a favor for an old man? I chuckle, because Bill continued to memorize huge portions of Scripture for more than two decades after that evening.

I cracked the door open and looked out on a sanctuary that seated close to a thousand people. It was packed. I wondered, why are these people here? Were they just a bunch of friendly skeptics come to see if we could actually pull off a stunt like this? I know I was wondering if we could, the more so with each minute that passed before we walked out to recite from memory each one of the 11,995 words of that brilliant and opaque last book in the New Testament. Divided among the three of us, that would be 3998 words each. Yikes!

Well we did it. The audience sat in rapt attention for two hours. Even the children were riveted by the story, the hair-raising images and the weird beasts. When we finished with the final "The grace of the Lord Jesus Christ be with God's people. Amen," everyone practically jumped to their feet to give us, and I believe the Word of God, a standing ovation.

Stomping and Clapping and Cheering

I had never experienced anything like this. And I was to experience it again and again over the next three years. We repeated the Revelation "performance" a few more times, I don't remember how many. Then we moved on to recite before large audiences at the college and in churches, the entire gospel of Mark, and finally the book of Romans.

Something stunning happened when we recited Romans before Hope students in Dimnent Memorial Chapel. We were moving through the eighth chapter of Romans and Bill was now proclaiming, not just reciting, the last few glorious verses in the chapter, his voice gaining in momentum and passion as he repeated Paul's rhetorical questions from Romans 8:31–36 (NRSVA):

> What, then, are we to say about these things? If God is for us, who is against us? He who did not withhold his own Son, but gave him up for all of us, will he not with him also give us everything else? Who will bring any charge against God's elect? It is God who justifies. Who is to condemn? It is Christ Jesus, who died, yes, who was raised, who is at the right hand of God, who indeed intercedes for us. Who will separate us from the love of Christ? Will hardship, or distress, or persecution, or famine, or nakedness, or peril, or sword? As it is written,

> "For your sake we are being killed all day long;
>   we are accounted as sheep to be slaughtered."

And then, his voice thick with emotion and earnest, pleading authority, he declared the gospel truth:

> No, in all these things we are more than conquerors through him who loved us. For I am convinced that neither death, nor life, nor angels, nor rulers, nor things present, nor things to come, nor powers, nor height, nor depth, nor anything else in all creation, will be able to separate us from the love of God in Christ Jesus our Lord. (vv. 37–39)

When Bill finished, the brief silence that followed felt like an inaudible gasp. I prayed the students didn't miss any of the power of those words. I needn't have. Hundreds leaped spontaneously to their feet, applauding thunderously, cheering, and whooping amid whistles, giving God's Word a prolonged standing ovation. Some jumped up on the pews, stomping their feet as they cheered. I still get goose bumps when I remember it. They heard, really heard the transforming and enlivening truth and joy of the gospel. It was as though they heard it for the first time.

An Eruption of Gratitude

I remember another instance like that, told to me by a missionary. The stomping and the cheering and the clapping was like what happened to a primitive tribe in the jungles of East Asia when missionaries showed them the *Jesus* film. Not only had these people never heard of Jesus, they had never seen a motion picture. Then, all at once, on one unforgettable evening, they saw it all—the gospel in their own language, visible and real.

They were deeply moved as they saw this good man, Jesus, who healed the sick and was adored by children. Then the unthinkable happened! He was arrested and held without trial and beaten by jeering soldiers. As they watched this, the people were stricken. They stood up and began to shout at the cruel men on the screen, demanding that this outrage stop. When nothing happened, they attacked the missionary running the projector. Perhaps he was responsible for this injustice! He was forced to stop the film and explain that the story wasn't over yet, that there was more to come. So they settled back onto the ground, holding their emotions in tenuous check.

Then came the crucifixion. Again, the people could not hold back. This time they began to weep and wail with such loud grief that once again the film had to be stopped. Again the missionary had to calm them down, and explain that the story wasn't over yet, that there was still more. Once again they composed themselves and sat down to see what happened next.

Then came the resurrection. Pandemonium broke out this time, but for a different reason. The gathering had spontaneously erupted into a party. The noise now was of deafening jubilation! The people were dancing and slapping each other on the back. The missionary again had to shut off the projector, but this time he didn't tell them to calm down and wait for what was next. In a sense, all that was supposed to happen—in the story and in their lives—was happening.

God's Mirth

That was the air we were breathing during those days of revival at Hope. It wasn't as noisy and explosive as in that East Asian tribe—after all, it was in Holland, Michigan! But it was just as vivid and compelling. No matter the particular cultural expression, when God speaks, his "mirth roars in our veins and we are alive and enlivened."[61]

Over and over again through those years, students in chapel services would sing and clap their hands exuberantly, then pivot on a dime, and continue in the same vigorous spirit, hushed in silent reverence, to hear the Word of God preached. This occurred hundreds and hundreds of times during those years. And it continued throughout the week in the small group Bible studies that proliferated throughout the college community. The scene depicted in the Joel Schoon-Tanis painting, referenced in the first chapter, of students holding their Bibles in the air and shouting their confidence in God's Word, embodies as much as one scene can, the meaning of the spiritual revival at Hope College.

It wasn't that God hadn't been blessing the preaching of his Word before the revival. He always blesses his Word. But in times of revival he heightens the blessing and brings a breathtaking freshness to the words of the Bible. Ancient truth is experienced as new and as primal, even as raw as it was at the dawn of creation when God spoke his first word and light and life burst into existence. "In the beginning was the Word" (John 1:1), incarnate in Jesus Christ, and alive and active in God's speech. It has always been this way, and God's people have always cried out, "Glory be to the Father, and to the Son, and to the Holy Spirit. As it was in the beginning, is now, and ever shall be, world without end." Stone age tribes and New York sophisticates declare with one voice, "Amen!"

So we had found a place to stand. My staff and I were unabashedly copying the first Christian church, as described in Acts 2:42–47. Since those first believers in Jerusalem were devoted to four things, we, too, would be devoted to the same four: the apostles' teaching, the fellowship, the breaking of bread, and prayer. That was the place where they stood in a hostile world; that was the place where we would stand too—on the Word of God.

16

How Duct-Tape Man Sent Us on a Mission to India

Hill Geti Talk!

T his was the first, and probably a never-again-to-be-repeated event in Dimnent Memorial Chapel.

Before students arrived for the chapel service that day, we had hoisted a student high onto a rafter in the sanctuary's vaulted ceiling. He was in a costume covered entirely in silver duct-tape, dressed as "Duct-Tape Man," a superhero in a skit to be featured in that day's chapel service.

We liked to do skits from time to time because they were fun, and could be used to illustrate a spiritual truth, though it wasn't always clear what percentage was truth and what percentage was fun. This skit was really fun, and its impact would be big—very big.

The point of the skit and its "superhero" was that duct-tape can fix a lot of things, like broken chairs, leaky pipes, and bindings on old books. Just call Duct-Tape Man to the rescue. But there are some things that even duct-tape can't fix, like a broken heart or a guilty soul. Only Jesus can do things like that.

Our actor playing Duct-Tape Man was a student named Jeff Amlotte. Everybody loved Jeff, and I truthfully didn't know that Jeff was his real name until his senior year at Hope, because everybody knew him by his nickname "Spanky." As you may guess, with a nickname like that, Spanky was a lot of fun.

That day he would be grandly lowered out of the sky (the rafters) to a booming superhero theme song, step onto the stage, and be interviewed. We expected a packed chapel to roar its approval and that we would all laugh and be a little silly on our way to thinking about something serious.

I was so excited, I couldn't wait.

But my mood did a flip-flop, when people began to make their way into the chapel, and I saw a certain man sit down in the back row. I groaned when I saw that the man was an East Indian evangelist named Jesu Bandela.

We had expected Jesu to come visit sometime, and when he did we would have lunch with him after chapel. But we didn't know when. If I had known when he was coming I would have nixed the skit. Jesu was a devoted man of God who had suffered much for his faith in a land that is among the worst in the world for its persecution of Christians. His father had been martyred for his Christian witness. Surely, I thought, he would be baffled and offended by this frivolous skit. Surely, he would wonder about these shallow American Christians who would mix such mindless laughter with the sacred gospel his father had died for. Throughout the chapel service I was rehearsing, with continuous self-accusation, how to apologize to this holy man for our imbecilic behavior in God's house.

When we met after chapel, my apology was on the tip of my tongue. But before I could say a word, he shook my hand and hugged me, and nearly shouted, "That skit! It was fantastic! I loved it!"

I said, "You did?" and then, I caught myself and said, with a tone that sounded like I thought he would like it, "Oh! You did! Thank you!"

He explained that skits are very popular in Indian culture. Indians love dramas of all kinds and sizes. He related how, when the Coca-Cola Company first came to sell their product in India, every advertising and marketing strategy they tried failed. Then they learned about the Indian love of skits, and they started sending out teams of amateur dramatists to do skits on street corners everywhere they would sell Coca-Cola. By acting out little stories about their delicious beverage, it won the people over, in a big way.

Then he began to enthuse over the possibilities of Hope College students and chapel staff maybe going to India to preach the gospel using all the means he saw being used in chapel that day: music, preaching, and . . . skits! He waxed eloquent over how scores, maybe hundreds of colleges and high schools in India had been founded by missionaries. He said he had trusting relationships with many of these schools and their administrators. He explained how over the years the faculties and student bodies of these schools had become almost entirely made up of Hindus and Muslims, but that they still had Christian headmasters, and they still had chapels and chapel services when someone could lead them. What if those "someones" were us? What if he could sell these colleges and high schools on the idea of American college students coming to perform sacred dramas and liturgies in their chapels?

"What if? What if? What if?" soon became "Why not? Why not?" and before we knew it, "Would you guys come?"

I think he may have said all that before we ordered lunch.

It didn't take long to make a decision about his proposal. It all seemed so divinely arranged that our prayers for this possibility were not so much, "Should we go, Lord?" but "Is there any reason that we should not go?" All the chapel staff involved in the decision had a strong sense that traveling through India to declare the gospel was the right and propitious thing to do. So I told Jesu that we would go.

One detail we hadn't thought much about was that we would have to raise the funds to pay for the trip; a lot of funds. It was obvious that Jesu, which means Jesus in his native language, didn't have the means to pay for a team of Hope college students and their chaplains to come to India. But we were so giddy with proper confidence, we said to each other that if Jesu doesn't have the money, Jesus does! A friend of mine likes to say of God's commands, that whatever God orders he pays for. We believed that if God was commanding us to go he would provide the means.

My confidence was briefly shaken when I told President Jacobsen about our plans and asked for his permission to proceed. He listened carefully, frowned slightly and waited a while to respond. Then he asked a lot of questions about the trip proposal, legitimate questions, and finally said, "You may go but you may not do any fundraising for your travel expenses." He didn't want our efforts to fund a missionary junket to siphon off any money that might be raised for the college's general fund. Understandable.

I fear I may have sounded irritatingly cocky when I said, "That's okay. No problem. Thank you. We won't raise any funds, but God will." As I spoke, he had one of those, "Well, we will see about that" looks on his face—troubled skepticism tempered with curiosity. I didn't blame him. I'd been there too, when someone asked my permission to do something they said God told them to do, that God had not told me about. And I admit that there can be a fine line between humble trust and proud triumphalism.

It wouldn't be long before I wondered which side of the line I was on that day.

When I told my staff and the students about what the president told me, and what I said to him, their eyes widened a bit, but they believed me, in the same spirit they had when they prayed for God to fill the chapel with worshipers. And off we went, making plans, selecting a team and engaging in nonfundraising fundraising—also known as prayer. And it was happening. It was intoxicating to watch the money come in without asking anyone but God to provide. We felt we were living like the great George Mueller ʌristol a century before, who raised millions for his orphanages, never asking anyone but God for the money. When he told a British business-man about his radical method, the businessman was aghast and said, "Why you're living hand to mouth!" And Mueller smiled and said, "Yes! It's God's hand and our mouth."

I told the students and my staff this story, and others like it with relish until the deadline came when all the money needed for the trip had to be in. It was an all-or-nothing deal. As I recall we were $30,000 short. A lot of money had come in, but $30,000 was a lot of money too, and time was up.

It was a kind of faith crisis that I had never before experienced. It didn't trouble me so much that we might not go to India. What troubled me acute-ly was the trusting looks on the students' faces when I told them that God would provide. I was so sure that he would, so confident that he had given us the green light to proceed. I was as sure about that as I had ever been about anything like it. And it appeared that I was going to be wrong.

A prayer from Psalm 69:5–6 came to me, that I have often prayed since in many other situations:

> You, God, know my folly; my guilt is not hidden from you. Lord, the LORD Almighty, may those who hope in you not be disgraced because of me.

The night of the deadline, as I ate dinner with my wife, Lauretta, I ago-nized over the strong possibility that what I had been so confident of would turn out to be my folly, and those who trusted my words and hoped in God would be disgraced. Not only would I look silly, but they would be disgraced because of my foolish confidence.

When we finished eating, she said, "Let's pray about it one more time."

We knelt down in the family room to pray, and I'm not making this up; the moment I opened my mouth and prayed, "Our Father . . ." the phone rang. I got up, walked over to the phone, and heard a voice of the other end I recognized as a man in town I didn't know very well, but who I knew to be quite wealthy.

We exchanged pleasantries, and he said, "I hear you're taking students to India, is that right?"

I said, "Yes, it is."

He asked, "Do you need any money to do this?"

I said, "Yes."

He said, "How much?"

I paused and said, "We still need $30,000." I think the tone of my voice sounded more like a question than a statement—*Is this too much to ask for, to even mention?*

He said, "Hold the phone for a moment."

I could hear his muffled voice through his hand on the phone as he shouted across the room to his wife, "Is $30,000 okay?"

I couldn't hear what she said, but when he took his hand from the phone he said to me, "The $30,000 is fine. When do you need it?"

What God orders, he pays for. But he doesn't usually tell us how or when he will provide.

I love to tell stories like this.

17

The Light Shines in the Darkness

We were in India a few months later. Our group included Dwight Beal, Tim Heneveld, Ben Lappenga, Megan Hicks, Josh Schicker, Dan Patterson, Dolores Nasrallah, Kevin Edlefson, Allyssa Wickman, Matt Youngberg, Marc Baer, Marty O'Connor, and me.

Our first outreach meeting was to be where Jesu Bandela grew up, in the "village" (his word) of Vijayawada, population one million, give or take a few hundred thousand. This was India. We spent the afternoon setting up a stage on an empty field at the edge of town, along with a generator, lights, and sound equipment. The evening program would include a lot of music, a testimony from one of the students, a skit, of course, and a gospel message.

As we worked, two things occupied our attention. One was the sky, heavy and virtually boiling, with dark rain clouds. A rainstorm would cancel out everything we planned to do. We were worried, but comforted by the second thing that caught our eye: a number of women praying fervently in the field where the evening meeting would be held. We were sure they were praying for the same thing that we were praying for. So as we worked to set things up we saw ourselves as praying with them for God to show his power and hold back the rain so we could preach the gospel.

When the sun went down, our lights came on, the music began and hundreds of people filled the field. The air was heavy with humidity. Rain seemed inevitable. Only God's intervention could hold it back and give us freedom to tell them about Jesus. We were praying in faith that his hand would hold back the storm, because whatever God orders he pays for. Next came the skit. The people seemed to love it. So far so good. Then came the testimony. The people leaned forward in rapt attention to hear a student testify of how difficult his childhood had been until someone told him about *Jesus Christ*.

Stop.

That was the first mention in the service of the name, Jesus Christ. At that very moment, immediately after the name, "Jesus Christ" was spoken, lightning split the sky, thunder clapped, and it began to rain, not torrentially, but steadily. The meeting was over, we thought.

But the people were not leaving. Jesu later explained why. While we had been praying through the day for it not to rain, the women in the field were praying for it to rain! They had been suffering from a drought and their crops desperately needed water. God had heard their prayers, and at the name of Jesus Christ the rain came. For us the rain was a disaster, for them it was a sign: Jesus is here! Now they were waiting to see what else Jesus would do.

We asked Jesu, what was next? He said, "Let's invite the people to come to the front if they want to be prayed for."

Then he addressed the crowd in their language, and invited them to come forward to be prayed for in the name of the One who controls nature. And that's what we did for the next two hours—pray for the people of the village, many of them standing barefoot in the mud the entire time, faces glistening from the rain. Some of us on the team prayed with the villagers, others of the team prayed for those who were praying. And we prayed for everything from physical healing to spiritual conversion, from cancer to financial needs to freedom from fear. There were confirmed healings. Some professed faith in Christ that night. I don't know how many, but Jesu's team followed up with the people who came for prayer, and as time passed he rejoiced over the changes he saw in people's lives.

Jesu was not naive. As an Indian himself, Jesu knew and understood the Indian people. He knew them to be extremely religious, given to syncretism, and prone to embrace and incorporate into their religious sensibility whatever spiritual reality "works" for them. Only time would tell what kinds of soils the seed of God's truth fell on that night. But the seed indeed fell and the church in Vijayawada was impacted. We had witnessed a dramatic outpouring of rain and the Holy Spirit, and we wanted to see more. That we did.

A trajectory was set that first night. In the weeks that followed we would continue to see the power of God dramatically at work in the spiritual darkness of India. We held evangelistic meetings with thousands of high school and college students across India, and saw many profess faith in Christ. The light shone in the darkness again and again, and the darkness was confounded. And we were having fun. We felt God's smile.

Our trip to Calcutta, now called Kolkata, several days later, was espe-cially memorable. Jesu had scheduled an evening meeting in the Kolkata Cathedral, where the nineteenth century Anglican bishop of India, Regi-nald Heber, had served. Heber was the author of the classic hymn, "Holy, Holy, Holy." Darnisha Taylor, director of the chapel gospel choir, had taught us a black gospel version of "Holy, Holy, Holy," which we sang that night as part of our outreach. What a sight it was! The cathedral was filled with school children, many tourists, and the current bishop of Kolkata himself, all singing together with arms raised in the refrain, "Praise him and lift him up," pumping up and down as though physically raising and exalting the Lord. The bishop's smile was so broad, one could barely see the rest of his face. The service was boisterous and hilarious in the most holy and serious sense of the words. Many lingered after the service to talk about the gospel message they heard that night. A group of Irish students who were touring India as part of a humanitarian initiative, stayed afterward and prayed with us to receive Christ.

Even more memorable, and of particular significance for our work at Hope, was a visit the next day to Mother Teresa's *Home of the Pure Heart* in Kolkata. Most Americans had never heard of her before Malcolm Mugger-idge's documentary (1969) and book (1971), *Something Beautiful for God*. Since then, her name has become almost synonymous in the minds of many, with the word "saint." She deserves the association. Among other things, but chief among them, was her ministry to the dying, who in some parts of Kolkata were almost like refuse amid the garbage in the streets of that teaming city. The *House of the Pure Heart* was a place where they could die clean and fed and loved and *known*, by the compassionate nuns who served there. If I ever doubted that a place of death could be full of light and beau-ty, even fragrant with love, I don't anymore. Not after my visit there with the students.

Muggeridge's title for his film and book, *Something Beautiful for God*, is more than appropriate, because it is reminiscent of the words of Jesus. He used "beautiful" to describe the act of a woman who out of love anointed him with costly ointment shortly before his crucifixion. When some of his disciples objected to this as a terrible "waste" of money, he told them to cut it out, because "she has done a beautiful thing to me" (Mark 14:6). Teresa and her sister nuns' extravagant love for the dying was literally something beautiful for the Son of God who said, "Whatever you did for one of the least of these brothers and sisters of mine you did for me" (Matthew 25:40).

The beauty we saw in the *Home of the Pure Heart* was made more beautiful by its sharp contrast with the ugliness we saw at the other end of the same block, a temple to the Hindu goddess Kali. The city of Kolkata is named after Kali, "Kol" being a shortened version of the goddess's name. "Kolkata" literally means something like place of Kali. Kali is terrifying even to look at, as she is the personification of the anger of the goddess Durga, the explosively wrathful mother of the universe. Though Kali's role is to eliminate evil, she is the evil of anger herself. The meanings associated with these two goddesses is complicated, but one thing is clear: Kali demands blood continually, and animals are sacrificed daily to slake her thirst. Flies swarmed around the blood-spattered altar in the front yard of the temple. The whole place stank of urine and garbage. Standing beside the altar was an emaciated filthy man, wearing only a loin cloth, with matted hair and eyes like black holes into a pit descending into mayhem. Clearly demonized, his cracked lips were slightly parted in what I can only describe as a wolfish, predatory even lascivious grin.

Standing beside him was a nicely dressed young man who was inviting us to come into Kali's temple for a tour. I politely refused to take the students into the vile place. It took some effort to do it politely.

Nevertheless the light shone in the darkness, just a block away, and the darkness did not overcome it (see John 1:5). The difference between Kali and Christ could not be more distinct and dramatic, even graphic. She demands blood, he gives his blood; she requires another's life, he gives his away.

My refusal to take students into the temple of Kali followed me back to Hope College. It came in the form of a rebuke from a woman on the college staff.

18

One Mountain, Many Paths?

(Pluralism)

My previous discussions did not take proper account of that whole aspect of Christianity which is uncompromising, ornery, militant, rigorous, imperious and invincibly self-righteous.

—Alan Watts

We are not living in a world where all roads are radii of a circle and where all, if followed long enough, will therefore draw gradually nearer and finally meet at the centre: rather in a world where every road, after a few miles, forks into two, and each of those into two again, and at each fork you must make a decision. . . . I do not think that all who choose wrong roads perish; but their rescue consists in being put back on the right road. A sum can be put right: but only by going back till you find the error and working it afresh from that point, never by simply going on.

—C. S. Lewis, *The Great Divorce*

I n the fall semester of 1998, after we came back from our mission to India, a Hope College administrator called to make an appointment. She said she wanted to talk about the mission trip.

She had a lot of questions, all legitimate. But they had a certain rhetorical air to them, a kind of *telos*, one question building on another to a foregone conclusion. When she asked me, "Is it true that you refused to take students into the Temple of Kali?" I knew we had arrived at the reason she wanted to talk. The "is it true" part gave it away. It was more an accusation than a question: It was "Why did you do such a thing? Defend yourself if you can. Why would you deprive students of such a rich educational experience?"

I told her about the degradation and the filth of the place, the sense of threat and darkness that hovered over it, the black holes of eyes on the man standing outside, the flies and blood on the stone altar, the stench, and the evil. Every pastoral instinct in me screamed to protect the students, to stay away, and to protect myself. The invitation to enter the temple wasn't merely to tour a cultural and religious artifact, it was a lure to *enter in*.

I hoped to help her see how wrong and deceptive that place and what went on inside it was; to convince her of the spiritual danger and confusion of the cult of Kali. She listened politely, with pursed lips, and asked a few questions, less for clarification than for more evidence. I knew I was failing to convince her. Everything about her body and eyes said she thought she was patiently and laboriously listening to the ravings of a bigot. I was getting tired. I'd had the same sinking, drowning feeling as a preacher when I was losing an audience: people falling asleep, looking around the room, checking their watches every few minutes.

Then she glanced at her watch.

"I have to go now," she said. "But I'd like to tell you a story before I go. May I?"

Relieved to not feel I had to try to do any more convincing, I said, "Of course."

With gleaming eyes (really), she began: "A large crowd stood in the foothills of a high and beautiful mountain. Rays of light were streaming from its peak. It beckoned to all to come to the heights and be blessed there. But how to get to the top, to the glory? There were a few maps, each claiming to show a different route. Some of the pilgrims took the maps, and started the journey. Others set out to forge their own way. Time passed. For some it was many years. But the day came when all who once stood together in the mountain's foothills now stood gazing at each other in wonder and joy at the top. They had taken many routes, but all arrived at the same blessed place, for the mountain was vast and there were many ways to get to the top."

When she spoke that last sentence, she sat looking at me silently and fiercely for an uncomfortably long moment to let what she thought to be the deep and incontrovertible wisdom of her parable sink in. Then she got up and walked out of my office.

I had just heard, for the umpteenth time, the "one mountain with many paths to the top" theory of the world's many religions. Or how religious pluralists explain their variety and competing truth claims. The pluralist announces, often with the breathless excitement of one who has just discovered that two and two do not actually equal four, after all—that voilà! all these religions are true, more or less! Ultimately, they are all really saying the same thing, more or less! Gazing through a glass darkly, as we all are, they are guiding us to the same place, to find God, truth, salvation, health, enlightenment, peace—whatever. There may even be different ways the same God reveals himself—or herself or whateverself or however many selves God is—to different people in different times and places.

The pluralist must employ great creativity and imagination to explain how this can be true logically, how religions which flatly contradict each other can at the same time be saying the same thing, or pretty much the same thing. But like a character in Daniel Taylor's novel about Bible translation, pluralists are good at this—they can "twist words and concepts like a circus clown making balloon wiener dogs."[62] I've seen them do it.

Though such a view is offensive rationally, it does have the appeal of seeming warm and accepting socially, because it sounds so open-minded and tolerant. For this reason, among others, religious pluralism was the reigning orthodoxy for many at Hope College and a significant portion of its faculty, along with its theological cousin, universalism. Pluralism says there are many paths to God. Universalism says that in the end the paths don't really matter, because God will get you to God, whether you want to get to God or not. Love always wins. All will be saved, Adolf Hitler along with Mother Teresa.

The same year I met with that woman, I got a letter protesting an evening of prayer for unreached people groups in The Gathering. The "unreached" we prayed for were the unevangelized of the earth, all who have not come to the saving knowledge of Jesus Christ as Lord and Savior. These people would, of course, include Muslims, Hindus, and Buddhists, some of whom are usually present to some degree in the college. The letter was copied to my boss, the college president, John Jacobson. It is "exhibit A" of where this kind of thinking can take one. The writer declared that,

> For a college that promotes itself as being welcoming of diversity, this sends a markedly hostile message to a segment of the population, particularly to students who have been actively led to expect otherwise.... Students who should be highly valued for the differing views they bring to Hope, broadening and enriching the collegiate experience for all students, are instead placed under tremendous pressure to convert and conform.... It is propagating not the love of Christ, but an attitude of loving intolerance, resulting in the further confusion and marginalization of a group of students already contending with the difficulties of being very much in the minority.

There was much to argue with in this letter, including other statements purporting that Muslims can "hardly be *unaware* of Christ's message." Hardly? The truth is most Muslims are abysmally unaware of what Jesus taught. Who would have told them? Certainly not an imam. If a Muslim is told anything about the records of Christ's teachings in the gospels it is that they are hopelessly corrupt and false, that the "Jesus" of the gospels is the invention of Christians, not the words of Christ. My guess is that the person who wrote this letter was as ignorant as a typical Muslim as to what is actually taught in the Christian Bible.

There was much more to argue with in this letter, such as the writer's contention that students from other religious traditions were marginalized and under "tremendous pressure to convert and conform." This pressure came allegedly from overly zealous and insensitive Christian believers. There may have been students like this at Hope, somewhere. But I did not meet one in all my time there. Not anywhere. Not one. What I did find were many earnest Christians who were so intimidated by being characterized as "intolerant" that they were afraid to confess their faith in Jesus Christ as the one true and only way to God. Which is to say they were labeled bigoted for believing what the church has always believed in all times and places—the faith of Scripture as summarized in the historic creeds of Christianity. When I arrived at Hope, I met one orthodox believer after another who felt marginalized for believing the historic Christian faith. This was a staggering and monstrous irony. If Hindus and Muslims felt "marginalized" in a college that claimed publicly to be rooted the historic Christian faith, what are we to make of a college community where those who hold to this faith feel marginalized?

But inadvertently, the writer raised the really big issue surrounding the spiritual revival at Hope College.

> For this pressure [for nonbelievers to convert] to come from their peers is unfortunate. For it to come from directly from the office of the dean of the chapel is, to my mind, highly inappropriate. . . . If there is a debate among administrators regarding under whose auspices and authorities the chapel functions, there is none among the students; for them, the chapel represents the views of Hope College.

Bingo. There you have it. That was the issue: the views of Hope College. What were the views of Hope College regarding the Christian faith? From its beginning, the spiritual awakening at Hope had a double edge to it—encouraging to some, enraging to others, resulting in great conflict. It was as though two powerful weather fronts, one cold, the other hot, collided, with thunder, lightning, and an earthquake. The collision was between "the historic Christian faith," which Hope had yet to define; and Hope's long-standing affair with what was known as the "middle way."

Earlier in this memoir, I wondered out loud, whatever happened to the name Samuel Zwemer? How could a man of his stature disappear so completely from the institutional memory of Hope College? It's beyond the scope of this memoir to trace the theological and historical currents that swept his memory away. But that it had happened is without question and that loss is clearly and inextricably linked with the Spirit's word that mere chapel attendance and Bible studies was not a big enough job. I knew that I had been called to preach revival so that Hope would once again be a light to the nations.

19

Demonstration at Dimnent Memorial Chapel

*For the time will come when people will not put up with sound doctrine.
Instead, to suit their own desires, they will gather around them a great
number of teachers to say what their itching ears want to hear. They will
turn their ears away from the truth and turn aside to myths. But you,
keep your head in all situations, endure hardship, do the work of an evangelist, discharge all the duties of your ministry.*

—2 Timothy 4:3–5

It is the truth which is assailed in any age which tests our fidelity. It is to confess we are called, not merely to profess. If I profess, with the loudest voice and the clearest exposition, every portion of the truth of God except precisely that little point which the world and the devil are at that moment attacking, I am not confessing Christ, however boldly I may be professing Christianity. Where the battle rages the loyalty of the soldier is proved; and to be steady on all the battle-fields besides is mere flight and dis-grace to him if he flinches at that one point.

—Elizabeth Rundle Charles (1828–1896)

It was bound to happen.

Then fault lines in the relationship between the chapel staff and certain factions in the college community had been widening and were eventually going to break wide open. I say "the chapel staff" but the tension was usually aimed at me personally.

The tremors began the first month of my public ministry with students. The first tremor can even be dated. It was September 27, 1994, when I was asked to speak at a faculty luncheon. The second was just a week or two later, after I prayed with students on "porn night." Before two months had passed in my first year, I was twice accosted by faculty who had issues with my theology.[63]

Don't Rile the Already Riled

All this happened almost immediately as I got started at Hope. Already the rumor and gossip mill was churning out dark "hints and allegations"[64] about my character and convictions. Dwight Beal, who led music in the chapel worship services, was approached in a local restaurant by a Hope professor who cautioned him about being involved with me. "Be careful, Patterson is a racist," he said. Animus toward conservative, evangelical Protestants like me is widespread in the academic world. It is virtually an article of faith that for so many academicians we are obscurantist, ignorant reactionaries.

I vividly remember one professor casting about to find a way to affirm my evangelical orthodoxy, but also to encourage me to take the students deeper and further. Translated: more like his own theology. He said, "What you preach is all well and good for young people. But when are you going to take them out of the wading pool into the depths?" In other words, when are you going to stop dumbing down the depth and mystery of the Divine with this "Jesus loves me, this I know" stuff? In his case it probably meant sounding more like Paul Tillich and less like Billy Graham.

I wasn't about to back off my convictions and tailor my preaching to his concept of "the depths." But I didn't want to unnecessarily rile the already riled either. So I determined, at least for a season, to avoid "hot button" issues like LGBT and be more of an evangelist than a prophet. I set out to simply preach the essentials of the gospel and the practical matters of Christian living for young adults. If I was going to be reviled, I thought, then let it simply be for preaching Christ and him crucified.

How naive of me. As things developed over the next five years, the simple gospel was more than enough to rile the riled.

A Full Scale Earthquake

I was also going to learn that just preaching a simple, stripped down, bare bones gospel can be an elusive quest. "Christianity . . . , if false, is of *no* importance," wrote C. S. Lewis, "and, if true, of infinite importance. The one thing it cannot be is moderately important."[65] An infinitely important faith necessarily has infinite implications. Abraham Kuyper spoke the truth when he said that there is not one square inch of creation on which Christ does not lay his hand and say, "Mine."

This, of course, includes sexuality. It has always been one of the most contested "square inches" of creation where usurpers have tried to claim ownership of what belongs to God alone. So as the tremors increased between the chapel ministry and sectors of the faculty over the years, it should not have surprised us when they erupted into a full-scale earthquake over matters of human sexuality.

It happened when a female student, slated to be a small group Bible study leader in the chapel ministry, asked for prayer. She wanted us to pray with her about telling her parents she was a lesbian, and intended to live as such. Would we pray that they receive and affirm her sexual identity?

She had been assured by key members of the faculty that this was a good thing to do, and she obviously believed we did too.

One of our chaplains met with her. Over a period of two or three long sessions, the chaplain listened to the student's story, and tenderly and patiently walked her through the Bible explaining that Scripture condemns homosexual practice as sin. Unconvinced, the student said she would announce her sexual identity to her mom and dad anyway.

So we had to explain to the student that for her to embrace an unrepentant and sinful life choice would eliminate the possibility of her being a Bible study leader on campus. Of course this stung the young woman. And though she didn't agree with us, she later said she was treated kindly and was never bullied or shamed. She understood that from our perspective she could not be a Bible study leader in campus ministry. She didn't agree with our perspective, but she respected our convictions.

So she stepped down.

There were many reasons for all involved in this to grieve—both for the student, but also for the chapel staff. It was an embarrassing and acutely painful, troublesome process for her personally. She was sad, and we were sad too.

Not Who You Think You Are, But What You Do

There were other reasons for sorrow.

First and paramount, we grieved the choice itself and the corrosive effect it was having and would have on the student's soul. In the words of Preston Sprinkle, she wasn't a problem to be solved, but a person, an image bearer of God to love. The duality of the sexes is integral to the *imago Dei*, to be expressed only in the covenant bond of marriage, one man and one woman. God made us this way in wisdom and love. Anything other than this is not loving and wise but destructive. In the language of the Bible, it is sin, and the wages of sin is death. It was for love that we lovingly opposed her.

Second, we grieved the noxious idea that she, and many others, saw her sexual proclivities as who she was, her identity as a human being. The Bible knows nothing of this. It uniformly condemns homosexual *practice*, not homosexuals as a kind of person. Homosexuality is never an identity, but a behavior. So it has been for most, if not all, of human history. Before the nineteenth century, the idea of sexuality as hetero or homo, and any number of other permutations as forms of identity and selfhood, was simply unknown. The label, historically, has always been attached to what people do, not worn as an identity.[66]

This error greatly muddled and inflamed the conversation that followed, if one can call it a conversation. Because now, what the chapel staff had done was more than just upholding an archaic legalism. It had mounted a cruel attack on a student's personhood—her very self.

Third, and ominously, we grieved the fact that she obviously had been counseled in an opposite direction than we had counseled (and this by influential members of the college community). I call that spiritual abuse. It was unconscionable. We had known for a long time that there had been a not-so-"underground" movement of revisionist thought, practice, and activism in the Hope community about biblical sexuality. It was as brazen and public as an unofficial movement can be and remain unofficial. I don't know how many, but over the years a significant number of students had been lied to as this young woman had. And some of the faculty had not only done the lying, but were themselves practicing the lie.

Television Cameras at Dimnent

We were all nervous about what might follow.

It didn't take long to find out.

But first a caveat. I do not believe homosexual practice, though unequivocally sinful, is the greatest sin. The same with all else it may point to in the many letters that have attached themselves to it—LGBTQ . . . etc. But it is one of the sins du jour. Great or small, it is one of the ways the enemy of our souls inserts itself. And therefore it must be confronted. I agree with what Elizabeth Rundle Charles wrote in the nineteenth century:

> If I profess, with the loudest voice and the clearest exposition, every portion of the truth of God except precisely that little point which the world and the devil are at that moment attacking, I am not confessing Christ, however boldly I may be professing Christianity.

Back to the story.

At the next weekday chapel service, we walked out of our offices and crossed College Avenue on our walk to Dimnent Memorial Chapel. There were television cameras from Grand Rapids massed at the entrance to Dimnent, a large crowd of photographers, a smaller crowd of demonstrators and a curious art installation behind the chapel. And of course, we saw hundreds of students walking by and through and around it all on their way to worship God.

The art installation featured a clothesline with several pairs of pants and underwear hanging upside down, with the crotch of each dabbed in red paint. The message was a protest against the ways sexual "minorities" are oppressed and abused by straight society. They saw themselves as one, as among racial minorities that have been persecuted in American history. Hence the bloody crotches. The college's dirty laundry was there for all to see! Arise you sexually oppressed! Clearly they bought into the error that they themselves as persons, deep in their sexual selves, had been mistreated. They needed this kind of self-righteous anger to justify disrupting the sanctity of the chapel worship service students were gathering to enter.

It was also clear that people of the furrowed brow, from the "underground"—who we now call the "woke"—had collaborated to make this happen. It would happen again.

I was sad for the student who had stepped down from being a Bible study leader. I doubt that she wanted anything like this public event to happen. I was sure that she was being used by the aggrieved activists.

I was also chastened. How had we failed her? Years before, when I first saw the opposition of the "stonewall" folk, I decided to avoid public confrontation as much and as long as possible, especially in my preaching. I hoped to buy time for the chapel ministry to be established and grow. My staff and I just preached the gospel and dealt in practical theology. We always spoke the truth to the best of our understanding, within limits.

He Never Told Them What Wasn't True

But we clearly had missed something if this young woman could assume we would be okay with what she was going to do. I remembered something a friend, a president of a Christian college, told me. A church she had attended had enjoyed the ministry of a fine orthodox and evangelical pastor for thirty years. After he retired, the next pastor the church hired turned out to be a heretic, an apostate revisionist. He was a disaster.

I asked her, "How could this possibly happen? After so many years of faithful teaching?"

She said, speaking of the former pastor, "He always told his people what was true. But he never told them what wasn't true."

That was it.

I've meditated on that sentence for many years since. It is true: you never really know that something is true unless you also know what can't be true if it is true. Philosophers know this as the law of noncontradiction. Simply put, A and non-A cannot both be true. A choice has to be made. Light can have no fellowship with darkness. Part of what it means to be a sinner is to wish it were otherwise, that we can have our cake and eat it too, that we can follow Jesus and at the same time willfully disobey Jesus. In C. S. Lewis's fantasy *The Screwtape Letters*, the devils know this about their human prey, and they make much of it in their efforts to despoil a human soul. Senior devil Screwtape advised his nephew Wormwood to exploit in his human quarry, his bent "to have a dozen incompatible philosophies dancing about together inside his head," at once.[67]

Something had to change in my preaching. It wasn't enough to say what was true. I had to do more, I had to be specific about things that weren't true, especially in regard to the distortions of biblical truth about human sexuality.

It was the right thing to do. It was the hard thing to do. But it was a good hard that got harder.

20

The Most Polarizing Person

So never be ashamed to tell others about our Lord. And don't be ashamed of me, either, even though I'm in prison for him. With the strength God gives you, be ready to suffer with me for the sake of the Good News.
—2 Timothy 1:8 (NLT)

You have no enemies, you say? Alas, my friend, the boast is poor. He who has mingled in the fray of duty that the brave endure, must have made foes. If you have none, small is the work that you have done.
—Charles Mackay

Ben, you're the kind of person who can split an entire congregation.
—said to me by a seminary professor my first year of seminary

Merely having an open mind is nothing. The object of opening the mind, as of opening the mouth, is to shut it again on something solid. Otherwise, it is more akin to a sewer, taking in all things equally.
—G. K. Chesterton

Things got nasty—or nastier.

The demonstration outside the chapel was just the beginning of a campus-wide eruption of anger and accusation. Tensions grew between me and the faculty, especially with the "stonewall" cabal within the faculty.

Tensions also grew between President Jacobson and the college trustees and me. Naturally, they were alarmed. They wanted to know, why all this rage and discord? What exactly is the problem between Ben and his critics? I answered the question one way, but the critics, President Jacobson and the trustees answered it another. They insisted on seeing the division and rancor as relational—the dean has a "people problem;" he needs to learn to get along with people who don't think the way he does; he needs to appreciate and celebrate the "rich diversity" of differing understandings of the Christian faith; he needs to live and let live, to agree to disagree.

Middle of What?

I saw the problem as theological, not relational. We were divided by ir-reconcilable differences about what we believed to be true about the Christian faith. That made conflict inevitable. And I believe it explained their resistance to my diagnosis. Their judgment put the burden on individuals and personalities within the college. My diagnosis put the onus on the college itself, its leadership and its unofficial credo, a vague thing called the "middle way." The motto was "Hold to the center." My question was, "Center of what?" No one would say. I argued that a center, a "middle" without specific content, a circumference, is an infinitesimally empty and small point, really a lowest common denominator. How could a college with no creed, no statement of faith in the classic sense, manage to have as vague a thing as "the middle way" as the touchstone of its religious identity? Middle of what, indeed!?

Question: What can possibly hold so much diversity together, especially if the diversity includes the heretical and the apostate? *Answer:* Keep the conversation going, give all outlooks an equal voice at the table. Above all, keep talking. The unwritten ideology is that the process, the journey is the main thing.

Therefore, two main things emerged in the season that followed the demonstrations in front of Dimnent Memorial Chapel. Naturally they both were studies. It's the academic way. Then, in true "middle way" fashion, there were conversations about the studies, and conversations about the conversations and then some mandated conversations around meals.

My staff and I were asked by the college trustees to do a self-study in the spring of 1998. It was to be a kind of internal review of our programs and convictions. Addressing the conflict, I summarized for the trustees our convictions about the nature of the "problem" between us and our faculty critics:

Can we work with people whose beliefs are inimical to our own? We think we can when our differences don't come to bear directly on the things we are doing together. But we are honestly confused over how this can be done effectively. . . . We want to be as irenic as possible. But how? . . . It will not do to preach that we can somehow "rise above" these differences and peacefully coexist. That is the revisionist's sermon, and a self-serving one at that. Somehow hard choices have to be made. That, we believe, is the difficulty before the trustees and administration of the college.[68]

Understandably, this statement did not go over well with President Jacobson and the trustees. It must have felt like I had thrown down a gauntlet challenging them to see things as they actually are and do something about it.

That was probably my intent.

In addition to the chapel ministry's self-study, the college trustees also commissioned President Jacobson to appoint a team to do another study—an external review, that same spring in 1988. This study would examine the college community's attitudes toward the chapel program. The team was made up of experienced analysts, using a variety of methods including surveys, interviews, and focus groups. Their report was thorough, and when the results were released to the college community, all who cared to read it could get a pretty good picture of the fault lines dividing the college community and the work of the campus ministry staff.

Dinners Doomed by Definition

For my staff and me there were no surprises in the report. We already had a pretty good picture of what those fault lines were. We knew, going into the exercise, that generally the student body had positive attitudes toward what we were doing, and a significant number of faculty didn't like what we were doing. Though twenty-three faculty did sign a letter expressing strong support for the chapel ministry, most opinions ranged from slightly uncomfortable to kind of negative to really, really negative, and beyond. In short, the study's findings gave me personally an "astonishingly low" rating as dean, peppered with such adjectives as "immature," "intolerant," and, that old shibboleth, "fundamentalistic." But nothing new emerged. All the study did was provide metrics—numbers and percentages for these adjectives. I guess institutions like to collect data to quantify these things.

Then there was more conversation—a series of mandated "reconciliation dinners," where folks who had problems with me and my leadership could sit down and discuss them with me over a meal, maybe get to know one another. I thought, *Fine, let's do this thing. Let's speak frankly, let's call a spade a spade, and enjoy a tasty meal.* Nothing like that remotely occurred in any of them. All I remember about them was that the food was great and the conversation pallid and tentative. No one appeared to want talk about anything that might be controversial. I went home from these otherwise delicious meals with indigestion. The whole project was a miserable failure, based on a faulty premise of what the real problem was. It was doomed by definition.

Lord of Eternity

During this time, I was sinking pretty low emotionally. After one trustee meeting, I left thinking, "I'm toast. It's over for me here." I could see it in their faces. I was sure I would get fired. Later I learned that during this period President Jacobson had actually considered doing that very thing. When I got to my office, I sat down to read the mail on my desk. Disconsolate, I opened a package from a good friend, musician Fernando Ortega. It was his latest CD. It's title was *The Breaking of the Dawn*. What could be more timely in my darkened state, than the image of dawn breaking darkness! If that were not enough, the second song on the CD was dedicated to me and my family. It was *"Lord of Eternity."* It sang of the blessedness of a man,

> Who walks in Your favor
> Who loves all Your words
> And hides them like treasure
> In the darkest place
> Of his desperate heart,
> They are a light
> A strong, sure light.
>
> Sometimes I call out Your name
> But I cannot find You.
> I look for Your face,
> But You are not there.
> By my sorrows, Lord,
> Lift me to You,
> Lift me to Your side.
>
> Lord of Eternity,
> Father of mercy,
> Look on my fainting soul.
> Keeper of all the stars,
> Friend of the poorest heart
> Touch me and make me whole.
> If You are my defender,

Who is against me?
No one can trouble or harm me
If You are my strength,
All I ask, all I desire
Is to live in Your house all my days.

To receive that CD with that song and that dedication at that moment!
I prayed, "Thank you, Lord. You must really want me to stay with this thing!" The song, "Lord of Eternity," became the theme song for the rest of my time at Hope, 1998–2000.

Will You Stay If Ben Leaves?

One person who helped conduct the external study met with us to walk through the results. A discussion followed. The discussion was thorough, but there was something we didn't discuss directly. We spoke of the criticisms of the chapel program, but for most critics it was not the chapel program itself, it was me. I was the one under scrutiny; I was the problem.

Before the study was conducted, a member of my staff was actually approached by an influential faculty member who told her how much she and some of the other members of my staff were appreciated by him and his colleagues. He said, "We like you guys a lot. It's Ben we have a problem with. If it so happens that perhaps he is asked to leave some day, would you and some of the other people on the staff stay on?" She was appalled.

So when I thought all had been said that needed to be said by the external reviewer, I sensed by the pained look in his eyes that he had one more thing he'd like to say, off the record. After a pregnant silence, he looked at me, and then at the chapel staff sitting in the room, and then back at me and said, "Ben, I have to say that in all the years I have conducted studies like this, in a variety of institutions, you are the most polarizing person I've ever encountered."

I could see that it grieved him to say this. I wasn't sure exactly why. I knew he loved Hope College—was it because it pained him to see his beloved college so torn by division and acrimony? He seemed to be a kind man, maybe it saddened him to think he might have hurt my feelings, or to have embarrassed me in front of my staff, by what he said. Maybe it was all of the above. I wasn't sure. Even the walls in the room seemed to wince at his words.

But I was sure how I felt about being the most polarizing person. It had a lot to do with my sons, Dan and Joel. Both were students at Hope during my years as dean—Dan, the older, and his brother, Joel. Dan was an art major. In my experience people in college art departments often can be a little hostile and dismissive of those they imagine to represent a stick-in-the-mud conservativism—people like me. That Dan and I were so close and had such affection for each other was probably a mystery for some in his department. How could such a long-ponytailed, creative, edgy, avant-garde heavy metal fan be so close to his father?

"Yes, You Should Be Offended"

The year before the study, Dan went with a friend to a Halloween dance sponsored by the art department. Two things stood out that evening. One was another student at a microphone attempting to parody how I preach. Fair enough, Dan thought. But there were also three other people cavorting in the crowd, dressed in black clerical robes, wearing masks made from a blown-up photograph of my face. They wore signs, "The Pluralistic Ben Patterson." They didn't like my well-known critique of religious pluralism and my insistence that Jesus Christ is the only way to God.

Dan pointed at the three and asked his friend, "Is it just me, or should I be offended at this?"

She said, "Yes, you should be offended."

Dan is a big man, and when his eyes have that certain look, you don't want to mess with him. I'm sure his eyes had that look that evening, and when he walked over to the three, put his hands on the shoulders of two of the masqueraders, and said, "We're going outside," they went outside.

Then he told them to take off their masks. They took them off. The faces he saw were two people connected with the art department and the department secretary.

Then he said, "I don't have to defend my dad. But I'm a student here, and I shouldn't have to put up with my professors doing this stuff. You are going to take those masks off and leave them off the rest of the evening."

He probably said "crap" instead of "stuff." Or worse.

And they obeyed.

I Didn't Want My Family to Suffer

I was proud of my son and his courage, but it grated on me to see him suffer because of something his dad was doing. His college experience shouldn't be clouded by my unpopularity, I thought. And honestly, I was a little fearful that he, too, might find me ridiculous.

On another occasion, a professor conducted some kind of protest demonstration near the entrance of the dining commons, with me as the object of the protest.

As Dan walked by, he said something disparaging about what she was doing, like "Why don't you back off," and she shot back, something like "Why don't you do something about it?"

It wasn't a challenge to a fist fight, but for him to conduct his own counterdemonstration. But the atmosphere was volatile. I wasn't present to see this, but a witness told me that as she spoke, she moved very close to his face, too close, provocatively so, saying, "Why don't you do something yourself." I'm so glad Dan didn't lose his temper.

It wasn't typical for her to act that poorly. Even my biggest detractors were fairly civil publicly. But emotions were running high in that season, and sometimes things got out of hand, as when Joel got a phone call in the middle of the night, with a voice at the other end threatening to rape him homosexually.

Again, this father didn't want his sons to suffer this way because of what he was doing. I was afraid it would come between us, and turn them against me or the gospel or both. I felt the same for my dear wife and my younger children at home. Lauretta felt everything as keenly as I did, maybe more. When it came time for my third son, Andy, to go to college, the last place he wanted to be was Hope. My youngest, my daughter, Mary, seemed pretty untouched by the controversy, even as she immersed herself in learning piano from a fine Hope professor.

I didn't like being the most polarizing person, but I could take it, even embrace it. If Jesus bore the cross for the joy set before him, I wanted the same joy. If my hero, the apostle Paul, fought the good fight, I wanted to fight it too. I didn't want to sit on the bench; I wanted to be on the field.

But I wasn't ready for my family to suffer for it.

The One Person I Didn't Want to See

These were the thoughts, emotions, and misgivings swirling around in my mind as I walked out of my office on the day I was told I was the most polarizing person. I just wanted to keep my mouth shut and ponder. And I determined that I wasn't going to tell anyone in my family about the results of the external review, until I absolutely had to.

So who should I see walking toward me as I started to cross the street in front of my office? One of the people I most did not want to discuss the external review with—my son Joel, who cheerily greeted me with a loud, "Hey, Dad! How did the review turn out?"

We met in the middle of the street, and stopped. I looked down and tried to think of something to say other than what he'd asked me about. But the words "Not so good, Joel . . ." came out of my mouth, "Not so good, Joel . . . ." before I could finish, I broke down and wept.

And my son held me in his arms, as I sobbed, right there in the middle of the road.

We eventually had to get out of the street, and walk into a parking lot where I told him all about it, and he prayed for me. I had often spoken to others about the fellowship of the gospel, the communion of suffering for the kingdom. I had yet to commend it to my children. The thing I feared would come between me and my wife and my sons and daughter, or worse turn them away from the faith, has nevertheless become a bond with all of them, many times over. I should have seen that before, but I saw it that day.

Later, when I went to Westmont College to serve as campus pastor, Joel served with me there for fifteen years, as director of music and worship. Marked by the revival at Hope, Joel is a man of prayer and a gifted musician who discipled a whole generation of students as he led them in fervent worship of the triune God.

However, the nadir, the lowest moment of that season was yet to come. But it wasn't about me and my experience. It was about what I witnessed in Dimnent Memorial Chapel.

21

The Nadir

Nadir—noun: the lowest point in the fortunes of a person or organization.
—New Oxford American Dictionary

Error, indeed, is never set forth in its naked deformity lest, being thus exposed it should at once be detected. But it is craftily decked out in an attractive dress so as, by its outward form to make it appear to the inexperienced more true that truth itself.
—Irenaeus of Lyons (ca. 139–202 AD)

Your foes roared in the place where you met with us; . . . . they defiled the dwelling place of your Name.
—Psalm 74:4, 7

March 16, 1999.

I was used to seeing large crowds in Dimnent. Chapel services had been packed for five years, filled with people eager to worship the Lord and hear the Scriptures preached.

The Contra-Chapel

But tonight was different. For one thing it wasn't a chapel service, but a meeting convened to contradict and discredit what we had proclaimed in chapel services the week before. It was a contra-chapel gathering. The composition of the audience that evening included a large and vocal contingent of people, many from outside the college community, who came to hear and celebrate the evening speaker.

The speaker that evening was Mel White, a nationally known gay activist.

The week before we had conducted a weekend conference entitled, "Setting Love in Order." It was part of a chapel series on biblical sexuality, which featured Mario Bergner, an Anglican priest who had renounced homosexual practice because of his faith in Christ. His testimony helped us say what we most wanted Hope students to believe about homosexual practice. It is not the only sin, or the worst, but one of the many ways we can fall short of the glory of God. Our message was not a sectarian quirk, a narrow-minded prejudice. It was as broad as historic Christianity—what Christians have believed in all times and places for two thousand years. A soft spoken Anglican priest, Bergner brought a message of repentance, hope, and healing for those who struggled with unwanted same-sex attraction.

On A Roll

The organizers of the evening could not have found a more articulate and clever apologist for the opposite point of view. White had been an evangelical Christian believer, married to a woman for many years while a professor at Fuller Theological Seminary. He had also been a ghostwriter for Billy Graham, Pat Robertson, and Jerry Falwell. White and I moved in some of the same circles in the 1970s and had met several times in my work with the National Youth Workers' Convention and the satirical magazine *The Wittenburg Door*. We even interviewed him for the magazine. We weren't buddies, but we were friendly. That evening, the friendly part ended.

The last time I spoke with White was sometime before 1982, when he and his wife Lyla divorced amicably, and he came out as an avowed, practicing homosexual. He started "dating" Gary Nixon in 1984 and eventually married him legally in 2008. Soon after his divorce, he transferred his clergy credentials to the gay-affirming Metropolitan Community Church.

Significantly, for his role in the 1999 contra-chapel, White had been a prolific writer, speaker, and leader in the pro-gay cause nationally. He had published his autobiography, *Stranger in the Gate: To Be Gay and Christian in America*, in 1994). The next year he was appointed to be the National Minister of Justice for the three hundred gay-affirming churches of the Universal Fellowship of Metropolitan Community. In 1997 he was awarded the American Civil Liberties Union's *National Civil Liberties Award* for adapting the "soul force" tenets of Mahatma Gandhi and Martin Luther King Jr. And in 1998 he had founded the gay advocacy group *Soulforce* and had spoken at scores of colleges and universities, including Yale, Duke, and Texas A&M.

He was on a roll.

Scary Good

White was the big gun brought in by theological revisionists at Hope to nullify what we had done. Exacerbating the provocation, the organizers affixed the college seal to the lectern that evening. This was something we never did in our chapel services. The college seal wasn't necessary. Everyone knew this. We were conducting college business, leading Hope in worship. The organizers of the contra-chapel, wanted everyone to know that they too were conducting college business—official college business, real college business.

When White was introduced he walked up to the platform wearing a clerical collar, just like Bergner wore the week before. He made a few opening remarks, and then, with a mischievous grin, ceremoniously removed the collar, tossed it aside and stepped away from the podium. The symbolic message: "My collar is open, so is my heart. Let's be real. Let's talk heart to heart. Not like the other guy."

Though he didn't know where I was, he knew I was in the audience. More than once he baited me by saying things like, "Ben, you remember those songs we used to sing in Sunday School?" His message was essentially, "Ben, we come from the same tradition, you and I. I, too, was once blind but now I see."

When White was done with his presentation, I thought, "Damn, you're good, Mel."

Good at what? Good at what one should never be good at: making wrong seem right, making "error seem more true than truth itself" (Irenaeus). Ancient Greeks had a name for people who got hired to do this, usually in politics. They called them sophists. White was as clever and slick a sophist as I had ever heard. As he told his "story," he got us to like him, pity him, admire him, and even laugh as he breezily dismissed every passage in the Bible that addresses same-sex "love." In the end his personal story and desires were his argument, not his exegesis of Scripture.

He made all that the church for twenty centuries has believed and proclaimed for twenty centuries as the teaching of Holy Scripture on homosexuality look like just one big straw man. When he was finished he blew it all over with a flourish. Get serious, you literalists! Cast off your chains, sexual minorities! He had part of the chapel rocking like a Pentecostal camp meeting.

He sounded so plausible. He was scary good. I wouldn't want to face him in public debate.

When it came time for question and answer, White was in the groove. A significant portion of his audience was in it with him. Earlier, members of the audience were told that they could write out their questions on cards, and hand them to people who would select the questions for White to answer. Their job was really to curate the questions, and make sure the questions helped White advance his thesis. That they did. One lob after another to White—a crack of the bat, and the ball sailed over the fence to the delight of the fans. White was clearly having fun, basking in the adoration of his supporters.

The Striptease

And then it happened.

White was having so much fun that he grabbed the whole stack of questions out of the curators' hands and started answering them indiscriminately. Then he came to a question he couldn't resist. He was asked what he thought about pornography. He didn't just answer it, he delightedly waxed eloquent.

And graphic.

Here I must pause. I can't and won't use the exact words he used, but I can say exactly what he meant when he let us know he thought porn was for him just fine, even a pleasure to be enjoyed—in no uncertain terms. Then, drunk with the sound of his own voice, he went into some unsavory details about body parts, his and another's. All that without blinking an eye.

Give it enough time, cut it enough slack, and deceit will overreach itself. The psalms speak of people who fall into the pit they dig for others.[69] There it was for all to see, who would see. White had been wearing the attractive dress that Irenaeus said error wears to make it seem more true than truth itself. Then his whole presentation turned into a striptease. He was naked, and he didn't seem to mind what people could see.

Thus the title of this chapter: The Nadir. It was the lowest point of my time at Hope. The sanctuary of Dimnent had been violated and slimed.

Actually, it happened twice before.

The first violation was the demonstration enacted outside Dimnent after news got out about the Bible study leader we had to remove from our student leadership team. It was replete with the noise of newspaper reporters and television cameras, as students wound their way through the crowd, to enter the chapel for worship. Only a legalist could say that since the spectacle took place outside, the chapel was kept sacrosanct. But the worship service was violated at its point of entry. The same thing happened again on the weekend Mario Bergner spoke. Again, Christian worshipers were visually and verbally accosted as they entered the sanctuary.

Then came White's shameful pornographic discourse in the sanctuary, March 19, 1999. Though the worst of the violations, it was of a piece with its precedents.

I was beyond angry as I left the meeting that night—really too tired to be mad, just sad, discouraged, and emotionally spent. My wife, Lauretta, and I went home and sat silently by the fireplace in the family room. Then came a knock at the door, and another, and another as confused and discouraged students came to pray with us for the college. By the end of the night, the room was full of sober and praying students.

It was good to be together, and we were cautiously hopeful about what the chapel service would feel like the next day.

We arrived early the next morning, and when we walked into the sanctuary we were deeply moved by what we saw inside. A dozen or more students who had been in the meeting in Dimnent the night before were already there, quietly walking through the physical space, their hands gently touching its pews and walls, praying for the Holy Spirit to cleanse the sanctuary.

It Was the Perfect Thing to Do

I wondered what our chapel speaker, Dr. Timothy Brown, would have to say. Tim is a dear friend and at the time was professor of preaching at Western Theological Seminary next door. He had seen and heard the whole event the night before. What would he preach?

Tim also did the perfect thing for the occasion.

He didn't preach a sermon. Without comment, he just quoted from a deep internal reservoir the perfect Scripture for the moment: Matthew 7:15–29. Tim is really good at this sort of thing. He doesn't just recite Scripture, he delivers a text as though it was his own words. He marinates in the Word of God. I have watched him do this many times, with wonder. For me it was his best moment.

"Watch out for false prophets. They come to you in sheep's clothing, but inwardly they are ferocious wolves. By their fruit you will recognize them. Do people pick grapes from thornbushes, or figs from thistles? Likewise every good tree bears good fruit, but a bad tree bears bad fruit. A good tree cannot bear bad fruit, and a bad tree cannot bear good fruit. Every tree that does not bear good fruit is cut down and thrown into the fire. Thus, by their fruit you will recognize them.

"Not everyone who says to me, 'Lord, Lord,' will enter the kingdom of heaven, but only the one who does the will of my Father who is in heaven. Many will say to me on that day, 'Lord, Lord, did we not prophesy in your name and in your name drive out demons and in your name perform many miracles?' Then I will tell them plainly, 'I never knew you. Away from me, you evildoers!'

"Therefore everyone who hears these words of mine and puts them into practice is like a wise man who built his house on the rock. The rain came down, the streams rose, and the winds blew and beat against that house; yet it did not fall, because it had its foundation on the rock. But everyone who hears these words of mine and does not put them into practice is like a foolish man who built his house on sand. The rain came down, the streams rose, and the winds blew and beat against that house, and it fell with a great crash."

When Jesus had finished saying these things, the crowds were amazed at his teaching, because he taught as one who had authority, and not as their teachers of the law. (Matthew 7:15–29)

No comment. No comment needed. The Word was alive and active, sharper than any double-edged sword. It uncovered and laid bare the thoughts and attitudes of the heart, before the One to whom we must give account.[70]

No proverbial pin needed to be dropped to feel the reverent silence when Tim finished.

Nadir Postscript

Then I got this email, more than twenty years later. "Then" isn't exactly the word to use when the next event is two decades later. But that's only if time is measured arithmetically, by days and years. But it applies if the Greek word for time is *kairos*, instead of *chronos*. *Chronos* is time by numbers, *kairos* is time by season, what the time signifies. The *kairos* was . . . what shall I call it? . . . it was a time of spiritual warfare and struggle for the faith, of fighting the good fight for the Faith at Hope. Within the *kairos* of the nadir of the Mel White train wreck, I then received an email by one of the planners of that event, twenty years later, measured in *chronos*.

No exaggeration, she was the last person I expected to receive such an email from. A photo sums up the reason why. After the Mel White event, I saw it pinned to a wall in the psychology department office. It was of Mel White standing between two psych faculty, Jane Dickie and David Myers, a jovial, happy picture of smiling colleagues, perhaps even friends. There they were, the planners of the Mel White evening.

The email was from Jane Dickie. She has given me permission to print it.

Hello, Ben,

It has been years since we've seen one another and perhaps you, like me, are now retired. I retired from Hope College in 2012 after forty years of teaching and learning and being blessed by the community.

During the contentious years where you and I differed on many things, while at the same time united in Christ, I had a dream one night and I wanted to share that with you.

In the dream I was outside perhaps in the woods on our twenty acres outside of Saugatuck. I don't remember the specifics of the dream but I do remember God speaking to me saying something like, "This is my beloved child," indicating you. (Now don't be confused—I certainly wasn't—God was not naming you the Christ : -) But God was indicating to me that you mattered to God. I remember responding with tears in my eyes and asking, "Am I your beloved child too?" And then I woke up. It is a dream I meant to share with you all these years, because it was powerful. I've come to know we are all God's beloved, and that our care and compassion for one another is most important.

So with that, I hope you receive this as the blessing that I believe it is.

Peace and grace and God's love surround you today and all the days of our lives.

Jane

Some time after that email, when I was in Holland, we had a cordial meeting at a Starbucks, where I prayed the Aaronic blessing over her, and we hugged.

I'm including it because I think it belongs in this memoir. I'm not sure why, but I think it belongs. And I appreciate Jane's willingness to have it printed in my memoir. For whatever else she may be, she's a woman of strong convictions. In that regard, I'm a lot like her.

Without speculating on whether or not the dream was from God, and keeping in mind my strong conviction that she is terribly mistaken about some significant things, I can say two things. One, she seems to be someone I could enjoy being with as long as we didn't talk about really important things, things about which we are irreconcilably in disagreement. Knowing my penchant for laughter, I think we could have coffee again at a Starbucks. Two, it pleases and comforts me to think that perhaps the Lord may have actually given her such a dream about me. But wait. I can hear someone say, "Isn't your shared humanity the truest and most important thing?" To that I say, no, it is not. It is the holiness, goodness, and beauty of God that matters most. Get God wrong, and humanity goes awry.

Nevertheless, thank you, Jane Dickie. And may the Lord bless you and keep you.

22

A Vexing Question
(Any Regrets?)

Only a fool has no regrets.
—Dominic La Russo[71]

C onsciously or unconsciously, a vexing question has hovered over nearly every line I've written in this memoir.

The question is, *If you had those seven years you served at Hope College to live over again, would you do anything different from you did or didn't do? Do you have any regrets, Ben?*

I believe La Russo's judgment in the epigraph is true, and it troubles me. A good memoir should be a thoughtful reflection on what was and what is: what I remember about what I did and what happened; what I thought about it then, and what I think about it now. And above all, I should not make myself the hero of my own story.

Like an Icy Draft in a Hallway

I've put the question off to the end of this memoir because it is such a hard question. It demands that I revisit some painful and angry memories. I've needed time to think about it—a lot of time.

From the very beginning of my work at Hope, there were people who were peeved at me, sometimes furious. My Okie dad would say some were downright "spittin', cussin', and stompin'" mad, though usually just under the surface, sullen and simmering, and other times explosive. Maybe it just felt that way. I didn't, I couldn't, keep a head count of the aggrieved. Sometimes their anger was naked and out loud. Mostly it was palpable and understated, like static in a sound system, or an icy draft in a hallway, or the way it feels to enter a room full of lively conversation and laughter, and hear it suddenly go silent when you walk in. I had that experience more than a few times.

163

Here's an example of what I'm talking about. My wife, Lauretta, and I attended a faculty and staff dinner one evening, the occasion of which I don't remember. We sat down at a table with seats and place settings for ten. The table was mostly full, with two or three seats unoccupied. There were several politely terse introductions all around, the waiters brought our salads, and we began to eat. When I was about halfway through my salad, I looked up from my plate and noticed that everyone had left the table to sit elsewhere. It was just Lauretta and me sitting alone at a table set for ten. I don't remember whether we stayed or left the room and went to a McDonald's for dinner.

Downtown Holland, sometimes I would see a faculty member walking toward me on the same side of the street, and they would cross to the other side of the street when they saw me. This happened too many times for me to think it coincidental.

And yet . . . and yet there were hosts of people who loved me and deeply celebrated the spiritual awakening the Lord graciously brought to Hope College. With all the awkwardness and hostility I sometimes experienced, I'd do it again in a heartbeat, for so many reasons. Throughout my time there, I felt the Lord's love and pleasure in me. I saw a packed Dimnent Memorial Chapel, standing room only, students worshipping the triune God, exuberantly and joyfully, every time Dimnent's doors were open for worship. And it wasn't just students—there were people from all over the Holland community and region worshipping alongside the students. There was enthusiastic approval from many pastors and churches in town. Throughout those years, I witnessed great instances of God's redemptive power to change lives. And I saw the renewal of a vision for global mission for which the emigrant settlers had founded Hope in the 1800s, but over the years had all but died and disappeared. I had great friends, a covenant group of men who kept me sane, and that prayer and donuts prayer group I mentioned in the preface. And I'll say it again, I had a happy marriage to a woman who still delights and intrigues me, kids that I loved and admired. Did I say somewhere that I also laughed a lot? I marvel at how an atmosphere of struggle and hostility could be so mixed with hilarity.

A Spiritual Awakening or An Insurrection?

These were priceless pleasures, a resilient and resounding "nevertheless" amid the rancor already simmering in September 1994, one month after my public ministry began. The rancor continued to simmer barely beneath the surface for the next few years. and erupted publicly in my sixth and seventh years. From the beginning, it seemed that almost as soon as I opened my mouth, a sector of the college was offended.[72] What I saw as a spiritual awakening was seen by others as an insurrection. It was confusing.

All this discord was very hard and confusing for President Jacobson, the man who hired me. When he invited me to join his staff, I accepted it on the condition that he would pray with me for the college, once a week for my first year. He agreed, and our relationship began with a warm and gentle camaraderie, and grew into a genuine friendship of respect and joy as chapel attendance grew. Early on he said he felt the success of the chapel program was among his greatest achievements as Hope's president. A few years later, as he grew weary and frustrated trying to navigate the bitter controversy that surrounded my ministry, it was clear that he took little pleasure in me or my work. There were some tense moments between us, leading up to his retirement. From the beginning, I felt like a fish out of water sitting as a dean on the president's staff; by the time President Jacobson retired, it was downright excruciating. But from first to last John Jacobson was a kind and gentle man. I'm so sad it ended the way it did between me and this honorable brother. But I can't cannot say I regret the stands I took that caused the controversy on campus and led to the alienation between us.

We Knew That We Knew That We Knew

Hope's new president, Jim Bultman, had a lot to figure out about me too. When he came to Hope in the autumn of 1999, he had been the president of Northwestern College in Orange City, Iowa, for fourteen years. The college flourished under his leadership. Before Northwestern, he had been on the faculty at Hope College, where he had also served as a department chair, a dean, and a coach for seventeen years. Not only that, but he had also graduated from Hope in 1963. He was definitely an important part of the Hope family. Jim bled orange and blue, the school colors.

Bultman knew many of my critics at Hope very well, both as friends and colleagues. Their relationship went back many years. Me, he didn't know at all directly, except by reputation and that we had in common the same close friend, Ray Smith, the legendary Hope football coach.

What was he to make of this controversial and divisive dean of the chapel?

The new president may not have known what to make of me, but my staff and I were sure about what we thought of him. We had prayed fervently that God would make Bultman Hope's next president. And we were sure it would happen. One afternoon, after my staff and I had spent a day praying and fasting, I experienced a strong assurance in my spirit that Jim Bultman would indeed be our next president. As I did I looked up across the room where we were praying, and chaplain Dolores Nasrallah looked up at the same moment. Our eyes met and we both nodded a "yes" simultaneously.

How did we know this? We just knew that we knew that we knew. The whole staff agreed. I am imagining as I write this that for some readers this will sound what . . . silly? . . . delusional? I get that. I used to respond the same way to people who thought they had a "word" from God. And I still chafe when I hear someone pronounce authoritatively that God told them something. For my staff and me that day, what we heard was not something we were going to broadcast, but cause for a quiet confidence in God's mysterious providence. We could go ahead with our plans and ministry without fear.

Looking back on what followed, I was going to need that confidence more than anyone else on my staff.

The trustees had conducted a national search for the next president. Before Bultman was chosen, he was one of two final candidates brought to campus for interviews. All I will say about the other candidate is that he and Bultman were polar opposites. It was clear to me that if this other candidate became president, I would soon not be working at Hope.

My Most Miserable Season

Jim Bultman, thank God, was elected president, by what I later learned was a very slim margin.

Also, much to my surprise, thus began the most miserable season of my time at Hope. For most of the first year of Bultman's presidency I teetered on the edge of writing an angry letter of resignation.

What did he do? As he later told the college community, in his August 2000 presidential update, he put me under the strictest scrutiny of any member of his staff, in his twenty-six years as an administrator at two colleges.

In retrospect, I know what he did with me was exactly what he needed to do as a first-year president with a staff member many saw as incorrigible and a maverick. He needed to find out just who I really was to his own satisfaction. And he had to do it with rigorous and exacting objectivity to show the college community, especially my critics, that whatever judgments he made about me and my work at Hope, were fair and unbiased.

It was the right thing to do, and I hated it, mainly because I was so very tired of having to explain and defend myself. Add to that the fact that my expectations for a harmonious relationship with Bultman were extremely and unrealistically high because of what I perceived to be the depth of the common beliefs Jim and I shared. I should have known better. I had learned from my years as a pastor that common convictions deeply held are no guarantee of smooth relationships. When Jim put me under a microscope, my emotional reaction was to feel betrayed; I was exhausted, spiritually and emotionally from all the slander directed my way. And to be honest, I hate to be put under a microscope anyway, under any circumstance.

Swing for the Fences

Then he made a bold move. He asked me to reach out to my critics, take the initiative and be reconciled to them. Just like that—have a heart-to-heart conversation, shake hands and make up, bury the ax and be reconciled. The gospel simplicity of his request was refreshing, though staggering, and frustrating, because it smacked of the ongoing disagreement I had with his predecessor, my first boss, John Jacobson—and not only Jacobson but the Hope College board of trustees.[73]

So again, my first impulse was to resign when president Bultman charged me with a second go at reconciliation.

But Jim is a man of immense integrity and courage, without guile, and eminently likable. He was an athlete—he coached baseball at Hope for fifteen years before he went off to be the president of Northwestern College. So I was disarmed when he appealed to a baseball metaphor in a letter to make his point about me pursuing these reconciliation meetings. He said, "It is my impression that in baseball parlance, singles will not do it at this point. We need to hit some home runs. Let's make some good pitches and hit them out of the park!" In other words, it's late in the game, we're way behind, we need something big to happen, and fast. So swing for the fences, and be reconciled!

But it forced me to make another run at understanding my opponents. Jim and I have since become friends, though when he urged me to just do it, go and be reconciled, the future of a friendship seemed pretty dim.

So I was to meet with these folks, and swing for the fences. But I made a slightly more modest counterproposal: what if I met with my critics one-on-one and just listened to each one until I could say back to them, to their satisfaction, what they were upset about. Debate would be off-limits, not even an exchange of views necessarily, just quiet, respectful listening on my part, until they were satisfied that I at least listened to them, and at least understood their point of view. If reconciliation was ultimately the result, praise God. If it wasn't, praise God still; maybe some seeds of reconciliation would be sown, and someday the Lord would grant the increase.

For me, this really wasn't that modest a proposal. It was a pretty big deal. I still had to be willing to really listen to each one or be willing to be made willing to listen, since by now I was pretty mad at them too. I would need a lot of spiritual strength to do it. I prayed that I would be willing and able, and we set up appointments with each critic. Only God knows my heart, and how willing to listen I actually was in those meetings. But I gave it my best shot.

23

They Said, I Said

This, then, is how you ought to regard us: as servants of Christ and as
those entrusted with the mysteries God has revealed. Now it is required
that those who have been given a trust must prove faithful. I care very
little if I am judged by you or by any human court; indeed, I do not even
judge myself. My conscience is clear, but that does not make me innocent.
It is the Lord who judges me. Therefore judge nothing before
the appointed time; wait until the Lord comes. He will bring to light
what is hidden in darkness and will expose the motives of the heart.
At that time each will receive their praise from God.
—1 Corinthians 4:1–5

I care very little about what you think.

I don't care much about what I think.

All that matters is what God thinks, and he hasn't passed judgment yet.

That's the posture the apostle Paul took toward the conflicts, critics, and criticisms he encountered in the Corinthian church. Paul has been my model. I love the man. Innumerable times in my ministry his attitude has strengthened and encouraged me. The struggles I had at Hope were not the first, and they have not been the last.

I don't like being disliked, but it's okay with me. It's a lot better than trying to please and appease an opponent, especially one whose beliefs and behavior I believe is contrary to the faith. Nothing could be worse than that. Nothing.

Early in his tenure at Hope, Professor Jeff Tyler met with me to voice his disagreement about something I'd said about the faculty. It was a friendly conversation, and after a while it drifted on to other things. Then he abruptly said with a grin, "You don't care what they think, do you?" I paused and said, "No, I don't." We became friends after that. He called me his "breakfast conspirator."

No Such Thing as An Immaculate Perception

I am a firm believer in the reality of the doctrines of Original Sin and Total Depravity. Everything I do, even the best things I do, are tainted by my sinfulness. The besetting sins of someone like me are things like pride and self-righteous anger. A close friend chides me for having the gift of snap-judgment. I know that I do, and it's important that I cultivate a healthy skepticism about how I see my opponents. That is the hard part of ending this memoir: to remember and reflect fairly on what my critics said about me more than twenty years ago in those "reconciliation" meetings President Bultman mandated.

And the reader should know that when it was all said and done, I still didn't move an inch toward agreement with their criticisms. But I hope I at least listened well.

It was a rare and rigorous project, having those meetings. It's not often that two people get together for the purpose of a critic telling the criticized what the critic doesn't like about the criticized; and then the criticized saying back to the critic what the criticized heard from the critic, to the critic's satisfaction that the criticized really heard the critic.

Whew. The project was not only rare and rigorous, but awkward, like the sentence I just wrote.

It took about three weeks to do this. When we were finished, it seemed to me to be a modest success. Without exception, after hearing my summary of what they said to me, each critic told me that it sounded to them like I at least understood what divided us. Did we part with a big hug and pledge to be buddies? Hardly. But maybe we ended up a little less hostile and less suspicious of each other. Maybe the main thing about those meetings was that I was able to cooperate with the hopes of my new boss, President Bultman.

One thing for sure happened. I discovered that the things I heard in those one-on-one meetings amounted to a brief compendium of all the criticisms directed to me in my seven years at Hope College.

As I write about them, the temptation is enormous to be snarky and sarcastic, and to filter their polemics through my own polemic; to make them look worse than they actually were. If any of my critics who were in those meetings read this memoir, it would be interesting to hear how well they think I did. I ask their forgiveness in advance if they think I misrepresented them.

Immediately after each meeting, I took notes on our conversation. I didn't take notes during the conversations because I wanted to maintain eye contact and to visually convey that I was doing my best to pay attention to them. I thought the most important thing we did together would not be to merely understand an opinion but to experience an empathic connection, if that were possible. So, in each case, I wrote down what I heard a few hours after I heard it. What you will read in this memoir is not a transcript of what they said, but my memory of what took place, as recorded a few hours afterward. Hopefully the memory, though not verbatim, will be authentic and faithful to the critic's intent. This will be hard to pull off. What I remember and write about may turn out to be more a perception of them as opponents, than a factual account. Dominic La Russo's judgment still holds true: "There is no such thing as an immaculate perception." But I'll give it my best shot.

What They Said and What I Think About What They Said

The critics will remain anonymous, though for some readers their identity may be obvious. Their views will be in bold italics, my views and reflections in Roman type.

- I talked to twenty people before I agreed to talk to you. We all agreed, who does he think he is, coming here and telling us we needed a religious revival before he even got to know us? That was sheer arrogance.

What I believed when I first came to Hope College and still believe is that most of the church in North America is in need of spiritual renewal, not just Hope. The fact that he and his colleagues not only didn't see the need for revival, but were offended at the mere suggestion of revival was proof that they needed revival.

If I have a single text that most sums up my convictions about the need for spiritual awakening, it is C. S. Lewis's declaration in *The Weight of Glory*—what I read at the faculty luncheon September 27, 1994.

If we consider the unblushing promises of reward and the staggering nature of the rewards promised in the Gospels, it would seem that our Lord finds our desires not too strong, but too weak. We are half-hearted creatures, fooling about with drink and sex and ambition when infinite joy is offered us, like an ignorant child who wants to go on making mud pies in a slum because he cannot imagine what is meant by the offer of a holiday at the sea. We are far too easily pleased.

A sleeping person doesn't know she's asleep. A corpse doesn't know it's a corpse. The question implicit in all God's complaints about his people is, "Why spend money on what is not bread, and your labor on what does not satisfy? Listen, listen to me and eat what is good, and your soul will delight in the richest of fare" (Isaiah 55:2). He wants his people to actually "participate in the divine nature" (2 Peter 1:4) and to "be filled to the measure of all the fullness of God" (Ephesians 3:19).

- You've destroyed this community with your exclusivist, simplistic, "sheep and goats" theology. You wouldn't believe the number of faculty who are taking or considering taking early retirement because of the things you have done.

I thought about that for a while. As near as I can tell, Jesus had a "sheep and goats" theology. He even used the labels in Matthew 25. And the "goat" category was what he had in mind when he condemned those who choose their own way instead of God's way. Or when he spoke about the categorical division between believers and unbelievers.

This is just a ballpark estimate, and a conservative one, but in my thirteen semesters as dean of the chapel, I probably preached between 150 and 200 sermons. I can't think of more than maybe four times that I may have preached what might be termed a "sheep and goats" message. That would amount to about 2 percent of my preaching.

If anything, I didn't speak about it enough.

However, in one sense I am guilty as charged. The truth is I was "worse" than he imagined. I not only believed there is such a thing as sheep and goats spiritually, as Jesus did; but I also believed there is such a thing as sheep and *wolves*, also as Jesus and Paul did. And I believed that spiritually all three of those creatures—sheep, goats, and wolves—were present at Hope College, some in the faculty. The odd thing about this criticism is that I never said any of this publicly. Never. I thought it, but I never said it.

- I have to hand it to you. You did what you said you were going to do. I didn't like it, but you were honest and you delivered what you call a "revival."

I never once said that I wanted to bring, or in any way engineer, "revival." I didn't say it because I don't believe it can be done. Only the Holy Spirit can do that. I said I would pray for revival, and invite anyone interested to join me. I desperately wanted to respond to his backhanded compliment and say that things like the explosion in chapel attendance were God's doing, not mine or my staff's. Revival is a sovereign act of grace, not a program or a human production.

But I knew that to give God the credit for something he clearly detested, would inflame his anger even more. So I kept my mouth shut.

- It will take us twenty years to undo the damage you have done.

I was hoping it would take a lot longer than twenty years for this to happen. So far, so good. The last I checked, as I write this memoir, twenty-three years after I left Hope, the chapel ministry remains vibrant and muscular. And I have noted that this professor and cohorts have retired.

- The composition of the student body has changed radically since you came, becoming more and more conservative theologically. Enrollment at Hope is bound to decrease if your ministry takes hold.

On the contrary, according to the Admissions department of the college, enrollment has increased at Hope—not in spite of, but because of the chapel ministry.

- You marginalized many of us faculty, especially in the religious studies department, by making it clear you believed our opinions were contrary to biblical teaching and historic Christian belief. The mandate of inquiry in a liberal arts college allows for hospitality to disparate views of the faith, and for those views to be represented by the faculty.

I wondered then, and still wonder, who said such a thing about this so-called liberal arts mandate of inquiry and hospitality to disparate views of the faith. I couldn't find it in any official statement of Hope College's mission. But I was very aware of the students this particular professor and other faculty had led astray in the faith.

One student, a religious studies major, told me that from the start the chapel ministry was a disruptive force in that department. This same student and some others, published an underground satirical paper they named *The Sons of Argos*, after the many-eyed, all-seeing, insightful dog of Odysseus.

- This is a college, not a church. You're trying to turn Hope into a church or a Bible college.

Such a thing never occurred to me. And if it did, I'd never have the energy to try. All I ever wanted was to see students joyfully worship and serve the true and living God, whether at Hope College or at Michigan State—and their professors to join them doing the same.

- You're a homophobe.

I do not have a phobia, an irrational fear of homosexuality. I reserve the word phobia for things like my fear of snakes. That is irrational, they scare me to death for no good reason. As an orthodox Christian believer, I stand with what the church has held to be true for centuries—homosexual practice is contrary to the way God created mankind and therefore sinful. To believe this is anything but phobic, rather faithful and sane.

- You cover up your inability to get along with people by slapping theological labels on them (i.e., "heretic," "apostate," "revisionist").

I have tons of friends. Always have. But I do have a problem with heretics and apostates. My biggest argument with Hope College was with those who wanted to redefine those categories merely as relational issues, not the matters of life and death they really are.

- Maybe you should think about leaving Hope College for another, more suitable institution. You should see your time at Hope not as a failure, just not a fit.

Not a "failure," just not a "fit"? Was I naive to think that things like a full chapel, standing room only; the proliferation of Bible studies campus-wide, and a renewed interest in Christian missions comparable to the days of the Student Volunteer movement, were not ultimately my doing, but God's? It was *soli Deo gloria* beginning to end. Totally. And it surely suggests that what I was doing, was not remotely a failure.

- You're not collegial. You should have spent the first six months at Hope getting to know the faculty, to form friendships. It's hard to demonize a friend. You should have involved the whole community in the ministry. You should have worked with the faculty in carrying out the program, presenting different points of view—it would have brought a lively dialogue between faith and learning, and a greater variety of worship styles.

Although a minority, from the beginning, members of the Hope community did come forward to warmly offer collegial assistance in the chapel ministry. A group of us prayed together weekly throughout my seven years at Hope.

The "stonewall" encounter early in my ministry discouraged any inclination I might have had to involve the *whole* community in the ministry. I discovered early on that a significant and vocal part of the faculty held theological convictions that were fundamentally incompatible, even hostile to my own. Given their reaction, how well would the collegial project have gone?

Besides, these "stonewall" people were not dumb. They understood the fundamental incompatibility of our beliefs as well as I did, and for this reason their plea for greater collegiality seemed disingenuous. What they really wanted was equal time in the chapel pulpit. In the final analysis, cynical though it may be, I came to believe the dispute was as much about power as advancing the "lively dialogue" of a liberal arts college. I have often wondered if this cry for collegiality would even have emerged if the number of students voluntarily attending chapel had not been so large.

I didn't come to Hope to get their permission to do what President Jacobson hired me to do. In the early years of my ministry, before I came to Hope, I got great advice from my first boss and mentor, Louis Evans Jr. He told me not to spend too much time trying to win over naysayers; it won't change their mind, and it will take time away from the people who agree with you, and need your encouragement.

- There needs to be a greater integration of faith and learning. That means inviting more risky people to speak in chapel. A dean should bridge academic and religious life. Students have therefore become suspicious of faculty. Your staff should represent a greater diversity theologically in order to appeal to "mainline" Christians (Presbyterian, United Church of Christ, Episcopalian, etc.)

This objection represents a typical faculty misunderstanding of chapel—not as a service of worship but as an intellectual forum and roundtable. But my staff and I were all about worship, which is mainly why so many students wanted to be in chapel. I know some wonderful and faithful people serving mainline churches. My ordination is from a mainline church. But the mainline church is dying.

- You're extremely talented, you possess great charisma and the students love you. Your gifts are evangelistic and prophetic, not those required of a chaplain. A chaplain is a nurturing, helping, supportive and affirming person—of people as they are and where they are.

I thanked him for calling me talented and charismatic, and added jokingly, "But so was Hitler," expecting a chuckle from him. What he said was, "That's exactly my point."

Which reminded me of a letter President Jacobson got from a concerned alumnus who called me "Rasputin," a reference to the debauched Russian monk who exerted an evil and intoxicating influence over the royal family of Tsar Nicolas II, during World War I. Even my opponents blanched at this. But it does provide color to this memoir.

I'll stop there.

Any Regrets, Ben?

How these meetings came about is described in the chapter, "A Vexing Question." The vexing question was, do I have any regrets for the things I said and did? As La Russo said, only a fool has none. At the end of my season of conflict, did I turn out in any way to be a fool? Did those meetings with my detractors lead me to regret any of the things I said and did?

The answer is, I have no regrets about the policies I pursued and the stands I took. The Lord have mercy on me if I am a fool, if I shouldn't have led the chapel ministry in the direction and the ways I did. If I am a fool, forgive me, Father.

Did I always fight the spiritual fight prayerfully with the weapons of faith, hope, and love? Did I always strive, in the power of the Holy Spirit, to "demolish arguments and every pretension that sets itself up against the knowledge of God" (2 Corinthians 10:5)? Probably not always, for I am a sinner. My conscience is clear, but God only knows the truth.

I'll probably be thinking about this for the rest of my life.

24

A Surprising Finish

By the end of the academic year, spring 2000, I had jumped through all the hoops, and when I was done, I was satisfied that I did my best in those meetings. I was also pleased and surprised to find myself enjoying my time under Jim Bultman's leadership. At the same time, I was equally surprised and incredulous when I heard the Holy Spirit say firmly, "You're done now." This was not a welcome announcement. I thought: Really? After all this work you're telling me to leave? I loved Holland and Hope, and would gladly have pressed into ministry, family, and community life for the next season. Even with all the discord of my years at the college, Hope is easy to love. But the Lord's voice was so strong, and repeated, that I finally told Dr. Bultman I was going to resign before the fall semester 2000. I think he was as surprised in hearing it as I was in saying it. And he asked, "Where are you going?" I said, "I don't know, but I know I'm supposed to go." That's how strong the Lord's word was: "You're done now." Jim and I talked at length about this, and he wisely persuaded me to at least announce my departure the beginning of the fall semester, that I would be leaving at the end of 2000.

Things happened very fast after that. Out of the blue, Westmont College, in Santa Barbara, California, contacted me and began a conversation that quickly led to an invitation to become its campus pastor. This, too, was a huge surprise. I wasn't at all sure, when the Lord told me to leave Hope College, that it would mean serving another college. It took me quite a while to say yes to Westmont.

These two things happening in such rapid succession—God's call to leave Hope and his call to go to Westmont—it left me with a little emotional whiplash. Jim and I were in conversation about this the whole time. By the beginning of the fall semester, 2000, I told the college that the fall semester 2000 would be my last. It had been seven years exactly.

I am grateful to be able to say Jim Bultman and I have since become good friends. In his presidential update, fall 2000, he announced my departure:

In my twenty-six years of being an administrator, I have never supervised an employee as thoroughly as I did Ben Patterson this past year. Knowing the polarized positions of well-intentioned people on both sides of this issue, I was determined to be as objective as I could without being a pest. I am pleased to tell you that Ben was a very good sport about this. He listened carefully, willingly accepted my recommendations, and implemented them to the very best of his ability. I thank and commend him for that. At the conclusion of the academic year, I met with Ben to review this effort and justifiably offered him continued employment at Hope.

On different occasions during the course of the ensuing weeks, Ben shared with me he felt God was calling him to a new ministry in a different place. Initially, he did not know where this would be. Ben and I discussed this at length and bathed it in prayer. When he sensed that God was calling him elsewhere and then specifically to Westmont College in Santa Barbara, he was given the freedom to pursue it. Westmont is an excellent institution, and I wish for Ben much joy and fulfillment in his ministry there. I will miss him both personally and professionally and want to publicly thank him for his significant ministry at Hope College. Ben will be concluding his work at Hope during this fall semester.

Jim retired from Hope on July 1, 2013. A year later he came out of retirement, so to speak, to speak at a dinner celebrating the twentieth anniversary of The Gathering. His presence was regal. I will cherish to the end of my life the personal letter he wrote to Lauretta and me, November 1, 2014.

This marvelous ministry, birthed under your leadership, has been the answer to prayer for so many of us who yearned for a return to the noble mission which marked Hope's founding purpose. It would not have happened without you! You were clearly God's instrument in his marvelous plan to bring spiritual revival to the college. Your Esther-like presence for "a time such as this" was obvious to all of us who loved the college. The vision and commitment of the Boersmas, together with the fervent prayers of your team and a few key others which preceded the planning and implementation, enabled God's plan to unfold.... By God's grace and goodness... two big myths have been brought to irrelevance: (1) A Christian college on the brink of becoming secular can't return to the roots of its founding mission and

(2) an academic institution can't be really good and Christian too.... Hope is a special, Christian liberal arts institution—and one that is also fragile. Future leaders must be diligent lest the college stumble in the path which you so unswervingly prepared.

Somebody Say Amen!

And so my part of the work at Hope College came to a close. I had clearly heard the Holy Spirit's, "You're done now."

On October 5, 2000, just before I left Hope College for Westmont College, I spoke to the college trustees and other members of the student life committee. I was asked to reflect on my seven years as dean of the chapel.

Here are my remarks:

Late this December I will be leaving Hope College after almost exactly seven years of ministry. Seven years! Astonishing. But even seven years of anything at my age amazes me. Time flies when it is in short supply. But these seven years have seemed like fourteen, even a whole career, they have been so rich and fruitful; by far the richest and most fruitful of my life. I don't deserve such a blessing. It has been pure grace every step of the way to be part of God's sovereign and determined plan to glorify himself at this institution.

So the truest and best reflection I can make is this: *Thank you, Father. To God be the glory.*

- for a chapel packed with students engaged in white hot worship;
- for hundreds involved in small group Bible studies, Christian discipleship, and mission outreach;
- for generations yet unborn who will know that the Lord is God because of what happened to their parents here;
- for the peoples of the earth who will know the light of the good news of Jesus because of Hope students who will proclaim it to them;
- for a college wrestling with the question of what it means for Christ to be Lord of all of life, including the life of the mind; and
- for a chaplain staff of wonderfully gifted, loving, and hilarious people to share the work.

My part in this work is done. God has made me to be a pioneer, a trail-blazer. As I look back over the years I have been in ministry, I see a pattern of start-ups and renewals. To use Paul's image, I usually plant and someone else waters, but it is God who makes things grow (see 1 Corinthians 3:5–9). But though my part in the work is done, the work is far from done. May I encourage you to continue the work, by way of a few challenges?

Pray. Countless times over the last seven years I have met total strangers who tell me they have been praying for Hope College for ten, twenty, even thirty years. Whatever good has happened here in my time has been built on those prayers. We have reaped where others have sown. Please keep praying! The tendency of most institutions is toward secularization, what sociologist Peter Berger observes is the process by which religious practices lose their practical social significance. Something like prayer may be seen as good for one's interior life, but not terribly important for the ways a college does business. Resist that. The chapel ministry has been built on prayer. Why not build the college's mission on the same foundation? "Unless the LORD builds the house, the builders labor in vain" (Psalm 127:1 NIV).

Be Alert. There's war going on. Nothing new about that. For whenever men and women choose to follow Christ they take sides in a cosmic conflict, not against people, nor anything accessible to the five senses, but against the "rulers, against the authorities, against the powers of this dark world and against the spiritual forces of evil in the heavenly realms" (Ephesians 6:12). That is why we must pray and be alert—not paranoid, but alert; for until Christ's kingdom is complete and he is all in all, there are no neutral places or ideas anywhere in all creation. The world of ideas and of the life of the mind have always been hotly contested in this spiritual conflict, because ideas have such far-reaching consequences morally and spiritually. Since Hope College, as a Christian institution, has unique responsibilities in these areas, I urge you to be alert.

Be Ready to Give an Account. They are not written in my calendar, but I have two appointments that I must keep. So do you. I will die, and I will be called to stand before God to give an account of my stewardship on earth (Hebrews 9:27)—what I did with the resources and especially the people he entrusted to me. A college like Hope is entrusted with the precious lives of young people. What will it be like for Hope's trustees and presidents, its faculty and staff and chaplains, to answer to God for what we did with those lives? Will we be found faithful? Will God judge that we have told them the truth about God, the uniqueness of his Son, and the mysteries and responsibilities of human sexuality? Will he find that we have upheld the authority of Scripture? I pray so. Our Lord's sternest warnings have to do with these matters.

Let the Dead Vote. G. K. Chesterton called his famous defense of tradition, "the democracy of the dead"—the idea that just because people have died they shouldn't be stripped of their vote. I think that is especially true of a college and its founders. Albertus Van Raalte and his heirs, believed passionately that Hope College should be distinctively and explicitly a Christian institution, so much so that they originally designed it to train ministers, missionaries, and teachers. Though the scope of their original vision has since broadened in a way I'm sure they would applaud, the core theological beliefs that spawned their vision should remain the norm for Hope, especially with its professoriate. Can there be any doubt what their vote would be on this matter?

Somebody Say Amen! That's the title of an award-winning documentary on black gospel music, and a fitting response to the remarkable thing that has happened at Hope College the last four years. Did you know that our gospel choir has grown from 25 to 150, with nearly double that number auditioning last year! Besides being great fun, what that phenomenon has done is to enable the chapel to partner with the department of multicultural life. What a privilege! Next to holding fast to the faith that birthed Hope College, the most important thing this college can do is to open its doors to rich diversity—the multiple tribes and tongues and nations that are Christ's body (see Revelation 5:9–10). In fact, Hope will cease to hold fast to the gospel if it doesn't do this. Good things are happening. Somebody say amen.

Well That's It. I leave Hope full of the hope that God's plans are good for this school if it seeks him with all its heart (Jeremiah 29:11–13). He certainly seems determined to bless Hope, and I've been blessed to be with you in that blessing. I'll never stop praying for Hope College.

25

In Their Own Words

I n C. S. Lewis's fantasy, *Prince Caspian*, Lucy meets the great lion Aslan in a forest on a moonlit night. Aslan is the Christ figure in Lewis's story. Lucy first met the beloved lion when she was quite young, and though for years she has longed to see him again, she hasn't. Now she is older and she is thrilled to see him again—and amazed to see how much her childhood friend has grown.

> "'Welcome, child,' he said.
> 'Aslan,' said Lucy, 'You're bigger.'
> 'That is because you are older, little one,' answered he.
> 'Not because you are?'
> 'I am not. But every year that you grow, you will find me bigger.'
> For a time she was so happy that she did not want to speak.'"[74]

I am blessed to have been a pastor to thousands of college students, for twenty-five years—even years at Hope followed by eighteen years at Westmont College. Again and again, thousands of times, I have stood and watched with aching and tender longing as these precious souls for whom Christ died stream into a chapel service to worship the true and living God.

That's why what I saw and still see happening at Hope gives me such joy and confidence in God's future. What I saw in the nineties and continue to see to this day are thousands of students, like Lucy with Aslan, discovering that as they get older, Jesus gets bigger. This is happening at Hope! That is why I wrote this memoir.

It is dedicated to the generations to come who will know that the Lord is God because of what he did with those who came before them from 1993 to 2000. I think you will enjoy hearing a few of them tell their stories. They are all grown up now—the young people I met way back when are now forty-somethings! And oh yes, as I write this, I am eighty!

Jon Adamson ('97)

In March of 1994, I remember going to a late night Bible study in Kollen Hall along with six other guys. We were an underground group, since the spiritual life on campus was pretty moribund. It was what it was. That particular night, Ben came to join us, and it turned out to be porn night in a nearby room. So we had a prayer meeting together.

But Aslan was on the move! Though we had been living near to those who would scoff, the Lord seemed to be saying, "I've had enough of contempt." Things on campus really began to change. There was a profound change of energy spiritually as chapel's impact grew. Some naysayers were saying, "Oh, it's just a flash in the pan. Just lots of bells and whistles." But it was real change.

The preaching was bold and compelling and caused us to trust in the Lord. The morning chapels went from not cool and moribund to a place of holiness. In fact, it became not cool to miss out on the holiness people were experiencing in meeting God. The Gathering on Sunday nights was another place where the Scriptures were proclaimed boldly and faithfully. All of this came to a head in the revival nights of March 1995.

And, yes, I also loved the role of satire as some friends and I addressed the conflict surrounding the chapel staff and the revival. We published an underground paper that was a lot of fun.

Since my days at Hope, I've had a strong desire for other people to experience the same love we experienced. The fruit of the Spirit's revival has borne so much fruit since then. I'll never forget the impact of Bible memorization as Ben, Tim Brown, and Bill Brownson recited the books of Revelation, Mark, and Romans. So many sermon topics, anecdotes, and prayers imprinted themselves on me. I still say this prayer every night over my boys: "Jesus, I love you. Jesus, I trust you. Jesus, make me more like you." That and the Aaronic priestly blessing, with Ben's tone of voice still in my ears.

Everything that was present back then has bloomed and put down roots. I saw then a total dedication to Jesus, all of our talents being used by him. I still follow the rule of St. Benedict in what I do in my job as director of the historic Cedar Grove Cemetery at Notre Dame University. In my waiting, in suffering, in patience, I try to find ways to offer my work to the Lord in prayer. I try to show a fulsome presentation of the gospel to those around me, availing myself of God's mercy even as I desire their good. These don't come to me without the years at Hope.

Jon Adamson is a 1998 Hope College graduate. He married Hollie Maxfield ('97) in 1997 and they have three sons: Ben (16), Will (14), and David, (6). Hollie has homeschooled the boys all the way through to the present, serving as lead for homeschool families in their area. Jon has taken a more active role as the boys approach manhood. Jon has worked in various construction endeavors before serving the church—on a team in the Episcopal Church, as a lay preacher in the Anglican Church, and now in his conversion to the Catholic Church.

Stacey (Vlietstra) Beebe ('95)[75]

To be honest, I didn't even know Hope had chapel services until my junior year when I met a couple of the twenty or so students that attended them. In my senior year the college hired a new team to lead chapel. This included Ben Patterson, who was in tune with the Holy Spirit and passionate about sharing God's heart, and Dwight Beal who led in worship. Dwight understood the difference between just singing songs and true praise and worship. It didn't take long before the average crowd of twenty turned into an average crowd of four hundred.

During spring break, I went on a mission trip with some fellow students. We had a wonderful time of serving and growing, and during that time the Holy Spirit kept calling us to pray. In fact, on the fifteen-hour drive back home, we prayed the entire time for our school—for something that only the Holy Spirit could do! When we returned to school, we could tell that God was up to something big, but we had no idea what. We could feel the air filled with electricity.

We kept gathering together and praying. Two weeks later, on Sunday evening, during The Gathering we heard testimonies from some Wheaton College students, of what the Spirit had recently done on their campus. After they spoke, Ben invited anyone who felt so moved to respond to what they shared. We prayed and we waited.

Then one person bolted out of his seat and to the front, and confessed before the entire crowd a pretty serious sin. For a moment, we were all stunned. Then impromptu teams came up to lay hands on him and pray for him. Minutes later, another person came to confess, then another, then another. Soon there was a line out the door. This went on until two o'clock in the morning—people confessing, repenting, being prayed for. The same thing happened the next night and the next.

In the months ahead, I saw chapel attendance become standing room only, people crowding the aisles and out the doors. Worship and praise filled the city, and many local congregations were affected. The following year, the number of Bible studies and small groups that took place in the dorms was in the hundreds! In fact, decades later, Hope College is a completely different place. Ben and Dwight are long gone, but the chapel and Sunday service are still standing room only. Imagine all the students who have met God at Hope and have gone on to share him with others all over the world!

Kevin Edlefson ('97)

It was my frosh year. I didn't go to The Gathering that Sunday night because I had to study. About nine o'clock, my friend James Palmer burst into my room and shouted, "You've got to go to chapel right now!" Then he ran out. So I ran in the dark to Dimnent Memorial Chapel. But the first door I tried to open was locked. I tried a second, and it was locked. Then another, and another—they were all locked! The last door I tried opened. What I saw going on inside was stunning; students were confessing their sins publicly, and praying for each other. Throughout all this there was a quiet sense of urgency. It went on until past three in the morning.

Over the next three years, I saw a subtle change in the kind of students who came to Hope. More and more were there because they wanted to grow in their faith, besides just get a college degree. I remember a religion professor who complained about the essays many seniors were writing about their time at Hope: "All any of them want to write about is their spring break missions trips."

My senior year I was worried about my uncertain future. Ben listened to me for a while as I voiced my insecurities. Actually, I kind of complained fearfully. Finally, he said, "You know what your problem is? You don't really believe that God loves you and has a plan for your life." The light came on in my heart. That comfort has been foundational for my life ever since. I may not know what is next, but as Ben liked to put it, I'm "fundamentally sound." Everything that ultimately matters is taken care of.

Kevin Edlefson was an intern with Hope campus ministries in 1998, has served as a pastor for eight years, and is currently on staff with International Campus Ministries at Western Michigan University in Kalamazoo. He married Amy Miller ('99), and their three children are now students at Hope. He is also working on a historical novel based on the nineth-century Saxon poem "The Heliand" (Anglo-Saxon for "healer"). The idea was birthed in a class he took from Hope professor Dr. Jeff Tyler.

Amy Miller Edlefson ('99)

When I came to Hope I felt like an outsider in my home church. I am an artist, a creative person. It didn't seem there was a place for me in the church. Hope chapel was a breath of fresh air spiritually. The experience of being in a massive crowd of humanity in chapel, Monday, Wednesday, Friday, and Sunday was inspiring. I belonged there. I had a group of good friends in the art and theater departments—and we worshipped together in chapel!

It was so encouraging to not have to separate my faith in Christ from my love of art. I could be a lover of Jesus and an artist. I could dance as part of chapel and connect the big ideas of faith in the Veritas Forum.

When my personal life got complicated and shaky emotionally, Ben's wife, Lauretta, and history Professor Marc Baer's wife, Patty, spent a lot of time with me praying about my future—especially during the time Kevin was on the mission trip to India. The Baer home was a place of refuge as I faced an uncertain future.

In the years following Hope, I've discovered that church ministry can be challenging, especially for the wife of a pastor. The formative years at Hope have helped me learn to sit in quietness with God even in broken and divided places. Even when a relationship with God is interestingly complicated, I know God loves me. He is there.

Amy Miller married Kevin Edlefson after graduation in 1999. She was a classroom teacher for ten years, and as of the writing of this memoir is pursuing a PhD in curriculum instruction in early learning skills at Michigan State University. She and Kevin have three children. All are students at Hope.

Kim Ebright Falconer ('96)

During my sophomore year at Hope (1993–94), I joined an early morning, student-led prayer group to pray for spiritual revival at Hope College. We always put spiritual revival at the top of our list. The more we prayed together, the more my friends and I noticed that God was giving us a heart for our campus and a deeper longing to see the lost come to faith in Jesus Christ.

At that time I learned that pockets of others were intentionally praying for Hope in a similar way, some for years. I firmly believe that in answer to prayer, God brought Ben Patterson to Hope (winter 1994) and blessed us with an amazing campus ministry staff the following school year (1994–95). This included Dolores Nasrallah (who became my mentor and dear friend), Paul Boersma, Dwight Beal, and Dani Hadley. We students *loved* and thrived under their Bible teaching, contagious laughter, relational gifts, and commitment to pray for Hope College.

At the beginning of my senior year (fall 1995), Ben Patterson spoke at the fall retreat for the Fellowship of Christian Students. I still have the outline he distributed to each of us, entitled: The Case for Prayer at Hope College. In his words, his purpose was: "To make the case for prayer at Hope College as our most central and radical act to bring about spiritual, intellectual, and social change in this institution and in the world." His clear, timely vision provided the leadership and encouragement we students needed to better understand the role of prayer and to persevere in it—and to give God alone the glory when we saw answers to prayer.

It was incredibly exciting to be in chapel at that time. Students who had never dreamed of setting foot in a chapel service came to check it out. The gospel was preached. God's sovereignty over every area of our lives and over every department on campus was proclaimed. Vibrant worship was sung. Fellow students were being convicted of sin, turning from it, and demonstrating interest in following Jesus. Not everyone who attended chapel was impacted in these ways. But many lives were truly changed. It was clear that God's Spirit was at work.

Kim Ebright Falconer attended Hope College from 1992 to 1996. Originally from the Chicago area, she is currently living near Philadelphia. She says of herself, "I'm a homeschooling mom of six children, including one who has Down syndrome. And I'm married to my best friend, Ben Falconer, a faithful, prayerful, Presbyterian Church in America pastor who always makes everyday life more fun!"

Raeann Schoudt ('94)

First, I want to say that the amazing awakening and revival that happened at Hope was the result of so many faithful prayers being lifted even before I was at Hope from 1988 through 1994. I became a Christian in high school through a group called Young Life which was led by some amazing Hope students who had hearts for prayer. When I first got to Hope I found a little prayer chapel in the basement of Graves Hall where there were journals that contained the prayers of these and other faithful prayer warriors. This was also the place where I would meet to pray with others, many of whom were part of the college ministry at a church called Lakeshore Vineyard.

We began to pray through campus, taking prayer walks through the chapel regularly and praying as the committee began to look for a dean of the chapel. So, when one of my professors, Dr. Jenny Everts, excitedly told our little class who were part of that praying college group, that they had found a dean of the chapel, and that he had asked to pray with the president at least once a week, we were so excited! We continued to pray the God would bring the right people for the chaplain positions and the other staff positions. Several of us were blessed to be able to have lunch with the chaplain candidates, since they wanted feedback from students. I remember meeting Paul and Dolores and believing they were the ones that God had for the positions. Several of us even prayed in the prayer chapel while they were in their interviews.

Even though I graduated in 1994, I was blessed to be around for that beginning of God breathing new life into Hope College. We went from twenty to thirty people in the chapel three times a week, including community members and alumni, to three chapels and The Gathering, all of which were packed with people sitting on the floor.

We saw hearts being changed, repentance and restoration, and the love of Jesus spreading out all over the world as Hope College came to life again in him. Thirty years later, my prayer is that God would do it again! He is so faithful!

Jennifer (Smith) Lane ('00)

As the daughter of Ray and Sue Smith, I grew up all things Hope. My parents (and many others) had been praying for revival and were thrilled when my dad's longtime friend Ben Patterson became dean of the chapel. While I was still in high school, those prayers were answered, and I remember the impact of that initial event. I was drawn by the spiritual fervor on Hope's campus and knew that is where I wanted to go to college.

My spiritual life before Hope was grounded but largely legalistic and I resembled more of a Pharisee than a follower of Jesus. In those first few weeks of my freshman year, I remember attending chapel, The Gathering, and gospel choir. There was an almost palpable presence of the Holy Spirit, and I just wanted more. I became immersed in a community of believers who were excited about following Jesus, who were committed to studying God's Word, and who were committed to praying. The Bible came alive to me, and I saw prayers tangibly answered. It was like nothing I had ever experienced before and marks a pivotal turning point in my life.

Three aspects had a lasting impact on my life. First, Bible study with Dolores and other leaders. It was here I learned how to study the Bible, how to walk alongside others with vulnerability and humility, and how important it is to pray together. Second, gospel choir. It was here I learned how to worship God freely in spirit and in truth, and it forever changed me. Third, chapel skits. It was here I learned how laughter is another way to connect with others and with God. It set the tone for joy. Recreating, writing, and dreaming up skits for chapel with Dwight Beal was so much fun. Bringing Dwight's idea of Duct-Tape Man to fruition was epic and resulted in midnight runs to Meijer to create Spanky's famed costume from a sweat suit and an old bath towel for a cape before his debut rappelling from the chapel ceiling.

After graduation, I found myself in a difficult season of trials which could have crushed me if it hadn't been for the transformation God had done in my heart at Hope. Instead, God used those trials to refine me and teach me how to rely on Him in everything. I don't look back on that season with regret but with thankfulness, for God has given me the opportunity to walk alongside others in their difficult seasons offering the hope we have in Christ. I am just one example of how the revival at Hope set my path as a follower of Jesus Christ. God's work at Hope continues. I see it in the next generation as my son is now a student at Hope and benefiting from the same spiritual atmosphere I did.

Jennifer (Smith) Lane uses both her academic and spiritual training to help others find freedom in Christ from their eating and body image struggles by means of nonprofit work, recovery coaching, and her Bible study, written out of her own struggle.

Joel Patterson ('01)

So why were we singing camp songs in chapel, with hand motions, all set to a programmed keyboard drum machine?

Looking back, my eighteen-year-old self would probably have been at home in the naturally-prone-to-be-critical-of-chapel-music camp. After all, I had grown up around classical music, as well as some of what I thought was the best of rock and progressive.

The work of the Holy Spirit through the revival at Hope changed my perspective. It's not that my encounter with the triune God dulled or dumbed down my critical faculties. Quite the opposite: the long-term effects of the revival in my life bore fruit in deep reflection, a greater love of learning, and a much broader interest in the ways the church has worshipped throughout the centuries.

But the Lord did something profound in me, and something that I wasn't aware that I needed: He made me take myself less seriously.

Through the revival, I experienced a heightened awareness of my sin and my need for a Savior, and a greater joy in being united with God through Christ's blood than I had ever known. Coming to terms with those truths resulted in profound joy, a joy big enough to feel at home singing junior high camp songs as well as being brought to tears by Handel's Messiah. Both were true, and both were about the same God—and if anything was going to be a barrier to entering into worship, it wouldn't be the music—it would be my own hard heart.

I grew in worship in ways I could never have foreseen during those years, which led to fifteen years leading worship in a higher education setting, and a seminary education. But it all started with (sometimes silly) camp songs and learning to hold my musical opinions a little more lightly.

I am eternally grateful for the conversion(s) I experienced, again and again, in worship at Hope College during the revivals—and for Dwight Beal, who taught me what it means to worship with excellence, scriptural integrity, and unselfconscious joy.

After graduation from Hope, Joel spent fifteen years as director of chapel worship at Westmont College. He is currently in business with his brothers Dan and Andy, as artist blacksmiths making beautiful objects of original art and function at Santa Barbara Forge.

Brien Hills Cruz ('99)

There are so many things to remember about my time at Hope and specifically with Hope campus ministries.

The students came in droves to the MWF chapels and Sunday night Gatherings. Standing room only! The worship was angelic, transforming, and Spirit-filled. The message was full of truth from Scripture and always reminded us how God was preparing each one of us to be sent out into all four corners of the world! The ministries were always grounded first and foremost in prayer. That was always the bedrock. Prayer and more prayer!

Today the things I take away from that experience is most assuredly a love of prayer that expresses itself in my love of the Book of Common Prayer.

To be honest my experience at Hope was somewhat utopic, and I struggled a bit with withdrawal after I graduated. I missed everyone so much, especially my spiritual leaders. I didn't love the "sending out" part of my story there. I felt lonely. But as I look back on the last twenty-five years of my life in ministry, I see that God's plan was for many of us to land in many places across the globe doing many different, amazing kingdom-building things—reaching the next generation of believers with the same truths we received not so very long ago. Now it's our turn to scatter the seeds far and wide.

I didn't realize just how full circle this memory process would be for me. Hope is a distant memory safely tucked back in the recesses of my heart, but recalling these memories and their significance today is timely. We are beginning to launch our eldest child. Now it's me doing the sending. Arrows that will land who knows where, who knows how, doing who knows what. Hopefully they carry with them lots more freedom, way more love, and a greater knowledge of our Creator.

What a good God we serve! What a loving Father! Lord, may you continue to write our stories right up to our very end. Pour us out, every last drop.

I know when I die, I want my soul to have the hands of a farmer, worn and weathered from never taking them off the plow. May we be fully spent for you Christ!

Miguel Cruz ('99)

I came to visit Hope as a high school senior and was blown away when I visited a chapel service. I thought, *Whatever God is doing, I need to be a part of it!* And I came.

Matt K., Tim S., and I lived at Durfee Hall during that first year, and it was a fun, goofy time. But weekly, we had a time of Bible study and the Lord's Supper, sharing in a life of sacrament and Word and worship. We had extended times to pour out our hearts to the Lord and we felt the weightiness of God's glory.

I watched Ben, Tim Brown, and Bill Brownson recite large portions of Scripture, and I realized human brains can memorize! So, I began to memorize 1 John, then Ephesians, then the whole New Testament. I loved the Summer of Service, and its rhythm of classes, solitude, retreats, and community. I saw their model of handling conflict, and it was huge in my growth.

I remember when Fernando Ortega came to sing at Hope, and I asked to use sign language to one of his songs. He graciously asked me to join him and that was the beginning of the Silent Praise worship group using sign language as a worship tool. I think it's still going on!

I loved being in Ben's sermon group, as he asked some of us to give feedback on his sermon for the week, and wrestle with the Scripture passage for the next. Through it all, the rhythms were being set for my life. The patterns of prayer, the Word, standing for truth, suffering and trials were being put in place.

I want to live by the truth of Psalm 86:11, with an undivided heart and with a singular focus: "Teach me Your way, O LORD; I will walk in Your truth; Unite my heart to fear Your name" (NKJV).

Brien and Miguel have been married for twenty-four years and have three children—Muireann (16), Fionn (13), and Lachlann (9). They have been in pastoral ministry, and Miguel was recently ordained as a priest in the Anglican Church in North America.

David Phelps ('00)

When I was a junior, my younger brother was paralyzed in a horrible car accident in which two other boys died. As I sat that night at the hospital, head spinning and heart crushed, the emergency waiting room filled with what seemed like my entire hometown—a very noisy, busy, annoying flurry of friends (God bless them) who had come to offer help and service to my family. I don't know how he heard, but Ben Patterson also drove over to the hospital. He sat next to me in the ER, and he said exactly nothing. He just sat with me. He was *with* me. After forty-five minutes of silence, he said, "It can be a lot of work to take care of the people who have come to comfort you." He patted me on the shoulder and left.

I could not recount for you a single line of a single sermon Ben preached while I was at Hope, though I heard scores of them and always left incredibly edified and often challenged. But I remember the sentence he spoke that night like it was yesterday. Beyond the canny and practical wisdom it contained, it said to me that here was a man with eyes to truly see what was going on, and that what was needed was not noise, advice, chatter, preaching, well-intended words that nonetheless offered cheap grace and cheap hope. What was needed was the real presence of God. Not a mere word, but a word incarnate.

That a man could see such a need, and make himself available, so simply and effortlessly, to let God provide for it—well, this spoke volumes to me that I am still trying to unpack in my own life. Apart from that of my own father, Ben's example—on that night most profoundly, and in other, more subtle ways in other times and situations—was perhaps the truest model—an image, form, and communication—I have seen of *fatherhood*. I saw what a man was. You don't unsee such a thing.

Generally, this sort of thing is my largest takeaway from my experience of Hope College in the 1990s as regards to the revival and the men and women who served God as our chaplains. It wasn't the worship music nor the preached words that accounted wholly for the Spirit moving as it did. It was the chaplains' *integrity*—that is, the *integration* in their very lives of the Word and the Word incarnate. Not just saying Christian things or making Christian promises, but *being* Christian.

Perhaps more precisely yet, it was the chaplains' *availability* to God, to let him use them as he would, to let him form them into what he would, despite the challenges they'd face and wounds they'd suffer. I can only account for it by believing that these were men and women who loved Jesus so much they were willing to suffer for it, so that from and through that wounded love, Christ could be present to his people. It's no wonder it caused (and continues to cause) a stir.

Later, as I contemplated becoming a Catholic, I went to Ben to seek his advice (and perhaps to be talked out of it). His counsel? You go where our Lord leads. If he is leading you to the Catholic Church, you follow him. So I did. And lo and behold, the real presence of our Lord, nascent in (for example) Ben's presence to my grief in an emergency room in Grand Rapids, took on an entirely new dimension. When I look at my children—one of whom is named after Ben—and see them know the presence of our Lord in a profoundly intimate way, I am flooded with gratitude for Ben's counsel. And now that I think of it, his counsel is oddly like that of the mother of God in the gospel of John: "Do whatever he tells you."

With hindsight, I understand another layer to Ben's counsel, a layer I saw he and his family and staff *live*: *be with* Jesus because he came to *be with* us. But when he comes, be ready, because he comes with the fire of love, and you'll either be purged and purified by that fire, or you'll be burned in your own passions, consumed by your own selfishness, lost in your own sins. Lord, have mercy on us.

At the end of the day, perhaps I might summarize my experience of Hope in the 1990s this way. It was as if we all—individuals, the community, the institution—were being asked the two questions our Lord always asks us: (1) "Who do you say that I am?" and (2) "Do you love me?"

As I believe was operative on some level at Hope in the 1990s, there is deep scandal to the question that is Jesus Christ, especially to those of us comfortable with our idols, and viscerally to those of us blind to our idols. After all, baser passions easily ignite when faced with the True Heat of God, jealous as he is for our love and suffering no competitors for it.

But I believe Hope's future, as my own, can only be truly anchored in some variant of the following answers to the two questions above: (1) "You are the Christ, the Son of the Living God," and (2) "Yes, Lord. Let it be done unto me according to your word."

My hope is that all of us from Hope continually rediscover the only place where hope is truly anchored: *Spera in Deo*.

David and Cheri Phelps have four children—Rock (a student at Grand Valley College), Perpetua (a senior in high school), Mary (13), and Ari (in junior high). David is president of Harmel Academy of the Trades, a postsecondary academy that trains men in skilled trades and forms them in their Catholic faith. The vision: "A Generation of Men of Integrity, Formed in Holiness, Skilled in Their Trade, in Solidarity with One Another and with Christ."

Jill (Pursifull) Nelson ('95)

Looking out across the Pine Grove from the Delta Phi sorority house in the center of campus at Hope, I would sometimes take note of the beauty of Dimnent Chapel. Even though I could appreciate the architecture from afar, it never occurred to me to enter those doors unless I had a class in the basement.

I grew up in a Christian home and professed my desire to follow Jesus when I was in fifth grade. I understood enough of the gospel to know that I needed Jesus to save me and that I wanted to follow him. But somewhere along the way, I got mixed up about how to do that. I started to think I could earn God's favor and so I tried to be a good daughter and a great student and to be really involved at church. That worked pretty well until another overwhelming desire snuck in there too. I found that the favor I really wanted after a while was the favor of my peers. And so by senior year, I was for sure at church on Sundays but I was also very likely also at the big parties on Saturday nights. I found that fun and connection fueled me (or at least I thought it did).

All this involvement wasn't bad on its own but it was the reason I was joining in stuff that wasn't really healthy. I was looking to define my identity and to do that I sought to please all the people I could. I wanted everyone to like me no matter what. So I believed I could be a good student who impressed my profs, a fun partier, and a pretty good Christian too . . . but over the years there was trouble ahead. The trouble started my first year at Hope when my father died unexpectedly of a massive heart attack. Later, when I was married, it came with a long struggle with infertility. Years later the trouble came with an aggressive breast cancer that resulted in a double mastectomy. Sometimes I felt like I was being erased.

Each time, God showed up in the deep darkness with his light, his mercy, and his grace. He met me in my deepest need and sustained me. And he taught me to love the Bible! Experiencing God's Word, actually reading the Bible for real and for myself was *the* game changer. God's Word is what changes people. During a time of desperate questions, I found a peace that I couldn't manufacture by having enough fun or connection or by making enough people around me happy. I found a God that was speaking daily and directly to me through his Holy Spirit in the words of the Bible. I found out that there wasn't a secret science to that. I found out that this wasn't just for super holy people . . . but this was for me, personally and every day.

Gazing out at Dimnent from the Delta Phi house, I could not possibly have guessed that I would one day be on staff as one of the chaplains of discipleship, in Hope's campus ministries. God's ways are not our ways, thank God! As of this writing, spring 2023, I am training seventy-six student leaders to lead small group Bible studies. The students in these small groups total five hundred.

And by the way, the site that used to be occupied by the Delta Phi sorority house, is now occupied by the campus ministries building. And the place where my bedroom used to be is now where my office is located!

Meg (Gustafson) Gregor ('99)

I was very involved in the chapel program during my years at Hope. I happily participated in several spring break trips, traveling with teams to New York City, Georgia, and Appalachia. I loved being part of SOS (Summer of Service) one summer and danced in chapel with the sacred dance group led by Maxine DeBruyn.

During my years at Hope the presence of God became so palpable to me. I know there was a lot of conflict, but I lived in the grace of God, in his presence. When conflict came up, it felt like we were all on a kind of high wire, but we had a guide that wasn't going to let us fall. I will always be grateful to Ben and the chapel staff for taking the stands they did, taking the hits that came with it, and persevering in love for us. The encouragement lasts to this day.

I think a trajectory was set back in those days, and I still live out of the convictions I came to during that time. The biggest is the power of prayer. For years, I've been leading prayer at my church in LA, and I know what a struggle it can be to persevere in prayer, even for a consistent fifteen minutes before every service. Then I hear Ben saying, "He is worthy. God is worthy of all our praise and prayer."

And I know my efforts are worth it, because he is worthy.

Meg Gregor graduated in 1999 and went on to get a PhD in 2010 at Harvard in biological sciences and public health. She delights in her two junior high children, Thomas and Esme, and is a lecturer in biology at California State University Dominguez Hills, where her husband, Brian, is a professor of philosophy.

Amy (Zwart) Bush ('04)

The chapel and Gathering programs were awesome. They helped me integrate my faith with my academic interests in science and math—there was no dichotomy between the two. Because of this the chapel ministry quietly became a recruitment tool changing the character of the college, as more and more prospective students were attracted to its vibrant worship and opportunities for spiritual growth.

Truth was spoken into my life by the sermons I heard. I learned to not be tossed around by whatever cultural winds happened to be blowing at the moment. Sometimes what was preached produced conflict in the college—but when does truth not rock the boat? My husband, Paul, and I are trying to raise our kids in a way that sets them apart from the world around them. Their middle names are Sophia, which means wisdom and Verity, which means truth.

The chapel ministry was reaching not only students, but the whole community—even people fifty-five and sixty years old! Though my dad graduated from Hope in 1971, he was so impressed by the vibrancy and student involvement in the chapel services, he made sure to get to one whenever he came to Holland on business.

God's plans, his love, his providence are so much bigger and wider to me now than what I knew back then. So also with my identity, which was so narrow. He is inexhaustible.

Amy (Zwart) Bush is married to Paul Bush, who was a senior at Hope when she arrived as a first year student in 2001. They later met during her senior year, were eventually married, and have two daughters. She has taught math and science for several years.

Paul Bush ('01)

I never wanted to miss chapel and The Gathering—they were so uplifting and moving and relevant. If I was late, I would sit in the aisles or stand in the back in the balcony just to be there. I didn't want to miss it! Chapel was a watershed event in my life, a place where I grew in my faith, and made it my own, not just my parents' faith. Things got started at Hope spiritually that continue to the present day. I still look daily for God's presence—and I find him. He's a personal God who meets me every day. After graduation, I came back to Hope to get a nursing degree, and still didn't miss chapel. For five to seven years after Amy and I got married, we still went to The Gathering. Even when friends came to visit they went with us to The Gathering. We were lucky—we didn't move away from Holland!

Paul and his wife, Amy, are raising two children. He works as a Nurse Anesthetist in Grand Rapids.

Mark ('98) and Jen ('00)

Mark:

I came to Hope College with a lot of ambition and the expectation that my Hope education would lead to a lucrative and high-status career. Although I had faith in Christ, it was not something that governed my every decision. I was a freshman just as Ben Patterson arrived, and I found the chapel services to be a source of spiritual growth in both intellectual and soul-moving ways, affecting both my heart and my mind.

The spring revival of 1995 was a further step in what God was already doing personally in my life as I was looking into ministry as a vocation and had a deeper love for studying the Bible. I wanted to be able to share God's

Word with people in the same way the chaplains were sharing with me. In the revival, I saw the power of the Word of God, public confession of sins, and the realization that all of us are broken in some ways. I saw that we each need the healing power of Christ, and the power of Christ working through each other.

Jen:

I also came to Hope with ambition and the excitement of attending an academically rigorous religious institution. I had heard stories about Hope's revival from a friend and looked forward to attending chapel and deepening my walk with Christ. I joined a packed Dimnent Chapel, filled with a desire to worship and learn. My heart was changed and drawn to serve Christ in an overseas setting. While I had grown up knowing Jesus, it was at Hope where I fully recognized that my faith should drive my vocation. I committed to serving unreached people groups during that time. Through the preaching and teaching of chapel services, on-campus Bible studies, and godly professors, my call was affirmed, and I chose a career in teaching English as a second language.

I met Mark in the fall of 1997, through an on-campus prayer group Mark had formed, using Operation World as a basis for praying for countries around the world. We also took the course "Perspectives on the World Christian Movement," coordinated by Barbara Yandell, and we were challenged to use our skills and talents in places where Christ is least known. Further years of seminary, teaching, and advanced degrees prepared us to leave for a Middle Eastern country in 2004.

We lived overseas for fourteen years while raising our sons in an Arab society and serving a language-learning institution. Coming back to the states for more education has been a challenge, especially during Covid, but this has brought us together as a family, as we adapt to an American culture. We have served in lands constantly in the shadow of political instability and persecution. We have faced many challenges with language, relationships, parenting, and finances. We are compelled to encourage ministry leaders around the world to send their best and brightest to the Middle East with full support.

Wherever we are, God's love compels us to reach out to hurting people. That love even compels us to follow Jesus's example and go seek out the lost. To quote C. S. Lewis, and an oft-repeated message from Ben, "We are far too easily pleased." The joy found in Christ, while serving and suffering for him outweighs any earthly blessing. While living in the states, we continue to serve the Arabic speaking community here and are also working with local churches to train others in being welcoming neighbors to new immigrants and refugees in their community.

Mark is currently in a PhD program related to missions. Jen is studying for an educational doctorate. Her focus is on teacher training for those who work with children who have refugee experiences. Our oldest chose to follow in our footsteps and is a student at Hope College. Our other two children are in high school. After completion of our doctorates, we will continue to serve these populations, wherever the Lord calls us.

Marie (Matchett) Wheaton ('97)

It's been so good to reflect on this! Every time I give my testimony, it's an opportunity to remember what has impacted my life.

I ran cross-country and track at Hope all four years. During my freshman year no one ever went to chapel—maybe a couple rows were filled. Then in my sophomore year, there was standing room only! I had never heard this kind of clear, biblical teaching before and got totally caught up in this movement. I went to a retreat where Ben was talking about the history of spiritual awakenings, and I had never heard anything like this before.

The faith of my childhood had been really shaken when I took a World Religion class at Hope, and the chapel staff helped me understand my confusion in some pivotal ways. I learned from Scripture that there was one way to salvation, and that mission service is the calling for every Christian. I felt a stirring to say *yes* to Christ by saying *yes* to Summer of Service, *yes* to going to Urbana Missions Conference, *yes* to being part of a missions prayer group (a.k.a. The MOB), and *yes* to a local church. I took the Perspectives on the World Christian Movement class with Barbara Yandell (and managed to get Hope credit for it).

As a child, I was taught about Jesus; at college my faith came alive; and as a wife and mother, I have been able to use my gifts to minister to the very real needs of other moms in playgroups and the homeschool community. The notion that Jesus wants my whole life has impacted me in every area of living.

My husband, Scott, and I are called to minister to the trekkers on the Appalachian Trail. In our twenty years together, we have used hospitality to offer friendship and truth to the many hikers passing through. We have trusted him for our ministry calling, for the four children he has blessed us with, for the simple life he has called us to. We want to continue to say *yes* by making sure we have the margins in life so that we can continue to minister to others and to be part of the local church—bringing people to faith who have never experienced a living faith. Scott and I pray that we'll never stop saying *yes* to the Holy Spirit in both big and small things.

Marie and Scott Wheaton live on the Appalachian Trail but only fifty miles from Washington, DC, with their children Lydia (16), Jonathan (14), Caleb (11) and Anna (7). They have been married for twenty years.

Christine Mutch ('96)

During my time at Hope, I observed and felt this palpable eagerness to experience the presence and guidance of God—and to do so in community. I have vivid memories of going to chapel in the Pine Grove or meeting up with my friends to worship in Dimnent. I remember attending prayer meetings with Ben before The Gathering where he taught us more about how to pray corporately and fervently, agreeing with one another and the Spirit in our longings.

So much of my growth came through the chapel staff, the ways that they embodied and exemplified the Spirit of God in their very being. It was vibrant and magnetic. Their intentional investment in students' lives was both caught and taught. I can still picture the room in Dykstra Hall where Dolores accompanied and empowered me to lead my first small group experience—one of hundreds I have led since. And I also have so many memories of just sharing life together—long walks around the streets of Holland, baking adventures (catastrophes?), meals with friends at our cottage, and the ways Dolores helped me to discern God's guidance in my life along the way.

My life and career have taken a lot of twists and turns in the decades since my time at Hope, but my pursuit of the presence and guidance of God in my life has remained a constant—whether it be discerning major career decisions, what chemo treatment to pursue when I was diagnosed with late-stage cancer, or how to help my own kids experience the nearness, guidance, and goodness of God in their everyday lives.

Professionally, I've served as a middle school teacher, college chaplain, executive leader, and pastor in a variety of faith-based organizations. Now self-employed as an executive coach and a learning and development specialist, my business is not explicitly Christian, and yet my faith informs my work as I draw out the unique beauty and divine DNA of my clients, help them be and do all that they were meant for, and overcome the hurdles that get in the way. In the process, I have learned that so much of the work of personal transformation happens in people when they simply create space in their lives to truly connect with themselves, with the Divine, and with one another.

The Spirit of God meets us in these places in profound and mysterious ways, whether people use that language or not. In many ways, I now see my job as an environmentalist who helps create and nurture these spaces, and it has been the joy of my life to journey with people along the way.

Jim and Marlaina (Kay Parsons) Rairick ('96)

Marlaina:

I came to Hope College as a student with a Christian background, but only vaguely aware of the ministry going on in the large and beautiful chapel. But that changed in 1994 when I joined a service in chapel and heard about a Hope student who had visited Wheaton College and had seen "something happening" spiritually on Wheaton's campus. After these Wheaton students came to Hope College to give witness, Hope students began talking about Jesus, confessing sin, and expressing repentance and faith in Jesus Christ. I was shocked that students were openly confessing sin; I had never seen or heard anything like it! My boyfriend, Jim, saw me as being both compelled and confused by this. As we continued to date, this season of attending chapel had an impact on me and caused me often to reflect on my own life and how I was seeing God at work around me. I continued to attend chapel weekly with my sorority sisters the rest of my junior and senior years at Hope.

Jim:

In the meantime, I was privately in a pretty disillusioned and miserable state for most of 1995, even as I planned to head for medical school. I considered chapel and Christianity personally irrelevant. I was not a Christian.

In early spring of 1995 my girlfriend's dad at their family gathering shared the gospel with me and talked to me about Promise Keepers. Weeks later I met a random man at a gas station who had a Promise Keepers T-shirt on. That same man took me to a Promise Keepers event weeks later at the end of my junior year at Hope College, spring 1999. I heard the gospel, was convicted of sin, and turned to Jesus Christ for forgiveness and true life. Pastor Tom Stark of University Reformed Church began to disciple me during my summer at MSU, then he connected me with pastor Tim Brown and chaplain Ben Patterson back at Hope when I returned for my senior year. I began to go to chapel, and experienced songs that celebrated the truth of the Bible, that rejoiced in the character of the Lord, and that engaged our hearts and minds to adore the Lord. Marlaina and I saw students coming to the Lord, including those who had called themselves Christians for years. We saw students who had been living in sexual immorality and drunkenness repent and turn around. We saw the aisles of the chapel lined with students in regular chapels as well as the Sunday evening Gathering. But our lives did not reflect this reality.

I didn't know the Bible, but I began to love hearing the teaching of God's Word. I vividly remember Ben Patterson quoting the Bible and talking about how he was seeking to let the Bible influence the way he thought and lived his life. I was gripped by the idea of teaching the Bible and living by it. What could be more important? I joined a group of young men who studied and memorized the book of Romans. I even remember writing out verses from Romans on small flash cards to carry in my pocket. I wanted to be ready when the guys would be quizzed by Ben! I learned to walk closely with the guys in the group, learning to confess sin and pursue godliness—a trajectory and disciplines that are with me to this day.

Marlaina:

In 1996, a year after graduation, I found myself talking with chaplain Paul Boersma about the "break up" with Jim and the double life I continued to lead. Paul guided me into a Bible study with other serious Christian women. It became clear that, though I knew about living a religious life, I had never come to the Lord in repentance and faith in Jesus. I experienced a true, life-changing encounter with Jesus Christ!

Jim:

I heard about Marlaina's true conversion and understood that my previous ways of relating had to change. After learning that love in Jesus serves people and does not use them, I learned over time how to treat a young lady in a relationship. Approximately a year later I told Marlaina, "I love you. Will you marry me?" There was a lot of "water under the bridge," and many people counseled us not to marry. We knew of each other's sinful activities in the past and had seen each other at our worst. But if Jesus truly makes us new, there is a new start and new possibilities. The old is gone. We are new creations in Jesus Christ.

After pre-marital counseling with Tom Stark and Ben Patterson, we were married in a beautiful and solemn ceremony officiated by both men on June 5, 1999.

Those who were lost are now found—that we, too, could become fishers of men. I have seen how I used to be the Lord's enemy, and now he has made me his friend. The Lord continues to make many his friends throughout the world, and we see how the Lord is sustaining his people to be a great witness throughout the world. The revival at Hope College is similar in many ways to how our Lord is at work throughout the world.

Jim and Marlaina served for five years at a college ministry at University Reformed Church in Lansing, MI. They then entered full-time service with Horizons International, a ministry focused on reaching the nearly one million international students in the US with the gospel and connecting them to local healthy evangelical churches. Globally, their aim is to reach Muslims with the gospel, and to bring theological and biblical training to the majority world Christians. Marlaina has worked out of their home, homeschooling their five children (three girls and two boys, ages thirteen to twenty).

She and Jim have partnered with the local church for evangelistic and discipleship purposes through hospitality and on-campus events. They have welcomed students from around the world, and have seen students saved out of Islam, Hinduism, atheism, and secularism. They have seen the saving work of the Lord in Malaysia, Indonesia, China, India, Nepal, Lebanon, Kosovo, Albania, Turkey, Bosnia and more.

Ben Buckhout ('97)

On September 10, 1997, a first-year student was tragically killed in a biking accident. His name was Ben Buckhout. He had been with us just three weeks. But he had already immersed himself in the life of the college.

Strangely, it seemed at the time, he and his father Don had biked together to college from their home in St. Paul, Minnesota. All that distance and no trouble; then a short ride around town, and the young man was dead. But I came to believe, and still do, that God in his mercy, gave a father and his son that particular gift before they would be parted.

The whole campus was shaken. I was shaken, in a very personal way, since two of my sons, Dan and Joel, were also students at Hope. Joel was in Ben's class. What if it had been Joel or Dan who died? How would I handle it? How could I speak into their death as pastor to their classmates?

The Buckhout family has a robust faith. Just days after Ben's death they came to campus and Don Buckhout asked if he could speak to the students in chapel. His words and his family's presence blessed the whole college with their clear witness to the hope of the resurrection. Don was especially courageous and clear about that hope.

A year later Don Buckhout was invited back to Hope, to speak to the student body again. He told us of attending the Christmas band concert at Ben's former high school, just three months after Ben's death. Ben had played in the band and had a special affection for that concert. As Don Buckhout sat in the auditorium that evening, and listened to the music, he was immersed in the special mixture of grief and joy only a Christian can know. "Where, O death, is your victory? Where, O death, is your sting?" (1 Corinthians 15:55).

When he walked outdoors after the concert, with the music resounding in his heart, he told us he looked up into a dark winter sky emblazoned with the dazzling light of billions of stars. And he said, silently, *Ben, I wish you could see what I see!*

Then it was as though he heard his son's voice answer, *Dad, I wish you could see what* I see!

The voice wasn't audible, it didn't need to be. It was clearly the voice of the Holy Spirit. What Ben's dad saw and heard that night paled in comparison to the glories of heaven.

The Scripture says that all the saints, those who belong to God, "have come to Mount Zion, to the city of the living God, the heavenly Jerusalem. You have come to thousands upon thousands of angels in joyful assembly" (Hebrews 12:22).

The joyful assembly of students at Hope, is part of a larger and more glorious assembly in heaven. When we began to worship in chapel, we didn't start the worship, we joined the worship.

Ultimately, Ben Buckhout didn't leave us and his family when he died. He just left what was available to our five senses. And when we come to that day when faith becomes sight, we'll realize completely, what Don Buckhout heard: *I wish you could see what* I see!

Epilogue
We Thought That It Was Because We Prayed

Then Jesus told his disciples a parable to show them that they should always pray and not give up.

—Luke 18:1

May the praise of God be in their mouths and a double-edged sword in their hands.

—Psalm 149:6

When the spiritual awakening came to Hope, many of us thought it was because we had prayed for an awakening. Certainly my staff and I thought so. But I discovered that we were only half-right about our prayers. Over the months of that first year I started meeting people who had prayed for decades that God would revive the college. Long before we arrived. Not only that, but I began to hear of people who died, having prayed for Hope's spiritual renewal, but never seeing it. The "we" who prayed was a lot bigger than I thought! Yes, our prayers were effectual, but they were a small part of a much larger chorus of intercession that had been going on for God knows how long. My staff and I didn't start the prayer meeting, we joined the prayer meeting.

I love to hear stories about instant answers to prayer, and I can tell a few of my own, but the truth is most answers to prayer come at the end of long periods of "waiting on the Lord," trusting that he has heard us and is accomplishing his good work in the way and the time that he, in his wisdom and power, deems best. But that's hard to do, and I have often had to turn to the pastoral wisdom of two nineteenth century German pastors, J. C. and C. F. Blumhardt, a father and a son, for encouragement. They wrote:

> Our prayers are hammer-strokes against the bulwarks of the princes of darkness; they must be oft repeated. Many years can pass by, even a number of generations die away, before a breakthrough occurs.

However, not a single hit is wasted; and if they are continued, then even the most secure wall must finally fall. Then the glory of God will have a clear path upon which to stride forth with healing and blessing for the wasted fields of mankind.[76]

Jesus said the kingdom of God is like the tiniest of seeds, a mustard seed, planted in the soil. It disappears and "dies" and then sprouts forth with new life when its time has come. It starts small, but with perseverance grows into a huge plant. Prayers down here on earth can seem weak and ineffective, even foolish. But their impact in heaven and then on earth is cataclysmic. John's vision of the impact of prayer in heaven is of incense poured on the golden altar before the throne of God, and then hurled back down to earth with fire from the altar, causing, "peals of thunder, rumblings, flashes of lightning and an earthquake" (Revelation 8:5; see vv. 1–5).

All this from the prayers of little people, unknown people, no account people. "History belongs to the intercessors," wrote Walter Wink, because they are, "those who believe and pray the future into being." God delights in this! That's because the weakness of God is stronger than human strength, and the foolishness of God is wiser than human wisdom.

To pray for God's kingdom to come is to look at the world and its tortured history from the highest possible vantage point. I read of a documentary that featured interviews and eyewitness accounts of men who had fought on the beaches of Normandy on D-Day in World War II. They were old men now, remembering what it was like. One man had fought on Omaha beach, where the casualties were staggering. When asked what he was thinking as he looked at the blood and carnage all around him, he said, "We're getting killed!" Another man had been flying a glider at thirty thousand feet on reconnaissance missions behind German lines, getting a glimpse of the big picture. When asked what he was thinking, he said, "We're winning!" The men on Omaha Beach couldn't see what the men in the glider could see. But what the men in the glider saw could only be seen because of the men on the beach—the persevering plodders.

Missionary William Carey is famous for saying, "Believe great things of God, attempt great things for God." It's a good saying, a heroic saying, inspiring and true. Not so well known was what he said to his father when he was a young man. When he announced to his family that God had called him to be a missionary in India, his father did everything he could to dissuade him from that venture, mainly by reminding Carey of all his weaknesses and handicaps. After this systematic dismantling of his self-esteem, Carey said quietly and firmly to his father, "I can plod." And plod he did, believing great things of God and attempting great things for God, often on "Omaha Beach."

A lot of "plodders on Omaha Beach" preceded my arrival at Hope College. I met one of them before she died. You probably don't know who Alice Vogel is. But God does, and Alice was one of the "unknowns" in Holland, Michigan, that my staff and I discovered when we came to Hope. She had the big picture, and she knew we were winning when she prayed with so many, some alive and some dead, for so many years, for God to renew Hope College. She barely lived long enough to see the renewal come, but she saw its beginnings before cancer took her life. I can only imagine how big the picture is she now sees in glory. I am thankful I got to join her in that prayer meeting.

Acknowledgments

Lauretta, my wife, chief editor, and writer-whisperer.
Where would I be without you?

My kids and their families

Dan and Leanne, Cor, Marshall, and Imre
Joel and Erin, Josie, and James
Andy and Mary, Oliver and Albert
Mary and Taylor, Ella, Thaddeus, Benjamin, and ? (on the way)

Long-standing friends and encouragers in writing

Ray and Sue Smith
Marc and Patty Baer
Barbara Yandell
Greg and Janet Spencer
Dan and Jayne Taylor
Kevin and Sherry Harney
Vijay and Jaylene Jayaraman
Reed Jolley

My Staff in those early years

Paul Boersma, Dwight Beal, Darnisha Taylor, Dolores Nasrallah-Sheveland, Dani Hadley, Cheri Beals, and Tim Hamilton

Fellow shepherds and stewards of revival

Jim Bultman
Tim Brown
Trygve Johnson

Dedicated pray-ers among many (you know who you are)

Herm Kanis
Adam Barr

Bill Brownson
Paul Bradford
Wednesday Morning Men's Group
Prayer and Donut Group
Saturday Night Prayer Group

Matt Scogin: student, friend, president, and lover of Hope College

Tim and Cheri Beals and Credo House Publishers

Notes

1 The state or period of being young

2 Charles Malik was a Lebanese Christian, a distinguished academic, theologian, and philosopher who served as the President of the Commission on Human Rights and the United Nations General Assembly. *A Christian Critique of the University* (Downers Grove: InterVarsity Press, 1982), 20.

3 A phrase coined by Dominick La Russo, a professor and mentor of my friend Greg Spencer.

4 James C. Kennedy and Caroline J. Simon, *Can Hope Endure?: A Historical Case Study in Christian Higher Education* (Eerdmans: Grand Rapids, 2005), 170.

5 See Romans 8:22–23; Galatians 4:19; 2 Timothy 4:7–8; Luke 13:24; Matthew 7:13–14; Colossians 1:28–29.

6 See Philippians 2:12–13.

7 See Luke 18:1–8.

8 See https://www.goodreads.com/quotes/180411-do-not-pray-for-easy-lives-pray-to-be-stronger.

9 A term coined by Dwight D. Eisenhower in his 1961 farewell speech as U.S. president.

10 See 1 Corinthians 1:18–25.

11 Indeed, the twentieth anniversary of The Gathering was formally celebrated by Hope College in September 2014.

12 P. T. Forsyth, *The Soul of Prayer*, (London: Independent Press Ltd., 1954), 14.

13 See chapter 2, "Remember When You Thought You Wanted to Work with College Students?"

14 See Romans 11:33–36; Mark 4:30–32.

15 An allusion to a spiritually defining moment in the life of Blaise Pascal which he referred to as "the night of fire." Pensees, 913.

16 Timothy K. Beougher and Lyle W. Dorsett, editors, *Accounts of a Campus Revival: Wheaton College 1995* (Harold Shaw Publishers: Wheaton, IL, 1995), 140–69.

17 See https://julieroys.com/days-long-revival-sweeping-asbury-university-in-kentucky.

18 An ancient Canaanite God often associated with child sacrifice.

19 See Matthew 13:24–30.

20 John Piper, *Let the Nations Be Glad* (Grand Rapids: Baker Books, 2010), 11, italics in original.

21 At that time, Hope College was called Hope Academy.

22 These stories come from the personal remembrances of his friend J. Christy Wilson, Jr., in *More to Be Desired than Gold* (South Hamilton, MA: Gordon-Conwell Theological Seminary, 1994), 107.

23 As quoted in Roger S. Greenway, *Brief Biography of Samuel Zwemer* (Phillipsburg, New Jersey: P&R Publishing, 2002), xi–xviii.

24 There was once a dormitory on the Western Seminary campus called Zwemer Hall, and there is a cottage on Hope's campus called Zwemer Cottage. But I've since discovered that those buildings were named after a different Zwemer, a James Zwemer.

25 John White, *The Fight* (Downers Grove, IL: InterVarsity Press, 1976), 216, italics in original.

26 2 Corinthians 10:3–5

27 "Unclubbable" was a term used by George Orwell to describe the unwavering courage of reformer Peter Damien, (ca. 1007–1073). To be "clubbable" was to be easily coerced into moral compliance and compromise by people's opinions. Cited by Os Guinness in Impossible People (Downers Grove, IL: InterVarsity Press, 2016), 32.

28 C. S. Lewis, *The Weight of Glory* (New York: HarperCollins, 1980), 26.

29 "God's Grandeur" by Gerard Manley Hopkins.

30 Cited in *Can Hope Endure?* by Kennedy and Simon from an interview with John Jacobson, 14 December 2002, 187.

31 See Romans 1:24; Colossians 3:5, 8.

32 See Romans 3:23; 6:23.

33 Irenaeus, *Against Heresies* book I, preface.

34 Matthew 8:28–34.

35 George Herbert, *The Complete English Works* (New York: Everyman's Library, 1995), 49.

36 Revelation 8:1–5.

37 Basil Miller, *Mary Slessor: Heroine of Calabar* (Minneapolis: Bethany House, 1974), 138.

38 C. S. Lewis, *God in the Dock*, ed. by Walter Hooper (Grand Rapids: Eerdmans, 1970), 157–58.

39 This was before the additional letters such as Q and + were added to the designation.

40 See Matthew 7:13–14.

41 James I. Packer, *A Quest for Godliness* (Wheaton, IL: Crossway Books, 1990), 22–23.

42 See John 17:20–23.

43 *2000 Years of Classic Christian Prayers*, Compiled by Owen Collins (Maryknoll, New York: Orbis Books, 1999), 67.

44 John Piper, *Let the Nations Be Glad* (Downers Grove, IL: InterVarsity Press, 2020), 22.

45 See Ephesians 3:14–19.

46 Frederick Buechner, *Telling the Truth*, (San Francisco: HarperCollins, 1977), 81.

47 J. R. R. Tolkien, quoted in Buechner, *Telling the Truth*, 81.

48 Augustine, *The Confessions*, 87.

49 See chapter 2, "Remember When You Thought You Wanted to Work with College Students?"

50 Mike Yaconelli and Wayne Rice were the guys I worked with on the magazine. Denny Rydberg took notes in the meetings. He later became the president of Young Life.

51 P. T. Forsyth, *The Soul of Prayer* (Grand Rapids: Eerdmans, 1916), 11–12.

52 "God sightings" was a whimsical phrase I learned from David and Karen Mains, a lighthearted way of speaking of the ways we saw and heard God at work in daily life.

53 David Wells, "Prayer: Rebelling Against the Status Quo," in *Perspectives on the World Christian Movement: A Reader*, ed. Ralph D. Winter and Steven C. Hawthorne (Pasadena: William Carey Library, 2009), 160.

54 See Matthew 21:16.

55 "One Name," Mark Altrogge.

56 It seems some very important things have happened to me on warm nights! See chapter 4, "Nights of Fire."

57 A phrase coined by James M. Kushiner in an article by the same title in *Touchstone* 33, no. 5 (September/October 2020).

58 "On the Reading of Old Books" in *Essay Collection: Literature, Philosophy and Short Stories*, C. S. Lewis (New York: HarperCollins, 2002), 16.

59 Lyle Wesley Dorsett, *E.M. Bounds: Man of Prayer* (Grand Rapids: Zondervan, 1991), 40.

60 Billy Graham, *Just As I Am: The Autobiography of Billy Graham* (New York: Harper Collins,1997), 139, italics in original.

61 Theodore Jennings, *Life as Worship: Prayer and Praise in Jesus' Name* (Grand Rapids: Eerdmans, 1982), 90.

62 Daniel Taylor, *Woe to the Scribes and Pharisees* (Eugene, OR: Wipf and Stock, 2020), 26.

63 See chapter 7, "We Will Stonewall You," and chapter 8, "A Prayer Meeting on Porn Night."

64 An evocative line that I like from a Paul Simon song, "You Can Call Me Al."

65 C. S. Lewis, *God in the Dock: Essays on Theology and Ethics*, ed. Walter Hooper (Grand

Rapids: Eerdmans, 2014), 102.

66 See Carl Trueman's *The Triumph of the Modern Self*.

67 C. S. Lewis, *The Screwtape Letters* (New York: HarperCollins, 1996), 11.

68 "Hope College Chapel Program Self-Study," August 1998.

69 See Psalms 7:15–16; 35:8.

70 See Hebrews 4:12–13.

71 Dominic La Russo was a deeply influential professor and mentor of my friend Greg Spencer during his days as a PhD student in rhetoric at the University of Oregon.

72 See chapter 7, "We Will Stonewall You," and chapter 8, "A Prayer Meeting on Porn Night." These chapters describe events that happened in September 1994, the first month public worship services began in Dimnent Memorial Chapel.

73 See chapter 21, "The Nadir."

74 C. S. Lewis, *Prince Caspian* (New York: Macmillan, 1951), 117.

75 Adapted with permission from Stacey Beebe's book, *Deeply Rooted,* (© 2020 by Stacey Beebe), 174–76.

76 Quoted by Rodney Clapp, *The Christian Century* 126, no. 25 (December 15, 2009), https://www.christiancentury.org/article/2009-12/waiting-room.